Living in Hope
and
Wisdom with Prayers

Heather Hope Johnson

authorHOUSE®

AuthorHouse™
1663 Liberty Drive
Bloomington, IN 47403
www.authorhouse.com
Phone: 1 (800) 839-8640

Published by AuthorHouse   11/20/2015

ISBN: 978-1-5049-6439-5 (sc)
ISBN: 978-1-5049-6446-3 (e)

Contents

Proverbs 4 vs 7

"Wisdom is the principal thing; therefore get wisdom: and with all thy getting get understanding"

Introduction

The Word of God states in the book of Proverbs:

"Wisdom is the principal thing, therefore get wisdom and in all your getting get understanding"

These words are key for us to live by, because the effects of sin are striking people from all angles leaving them hopeless, suicidal, lonely, angry, confused, bitter and desperate. In addition, the people of faith are being molested and disrespected because of their belief in Jesus Christ. We must not give up, but must continue to stand strong in grace, love and truth even while under pressure.

Do you know someone who is hopeless, prayer less or living a defeated life without the wisdom of God? These people are sensing an emptiness within and are crying out silently for help. The Lord revealed to me that some people who are materialistically wealthy, dressing the part, and living as if all is well, deep down inside they are empty because they are not filled with His Spirit. We were not created to live life alone. Many people think that they can manage life without help from the One who created them and so at times they become bitter and caustic about life and others. Many people believe that they can fill their lives with "things" in order to achieve happiness. Oftentimes they run to another human being for help, thinking that another person can be their 100 percent solution. No human being can be the 100 percent solution or answer to the issues in this life.

If you choose to put your full dependence in another human being, then get ready to be disappointed. It is not a smart or safe thing to do. Human beings get weary and tired and often quit on people who drain them. Instead, we must put our hope, love and trust in the Savior, Jesus Christ, the One who is able to help us especially emotionally and spiritually. It is not wise or considerate for us to put people under unnecessary pressure. Jesus carried the sins of this world, died for us and rose from the dead. Only He can bear our burdens. He said in the Scriptures that we can ***"cast our cares upon Him for He cares for us"*** If we cast our cares on another human being, we will undoubtedly get disappointed and often rejected when problems aren't solved efficiently. We are to put our hope in God, trusting Him to grant us the wisdom that we need to live. It is through a relationship with the Lord and His Holy Scriptures that will strengthen us to endure the storms of life.

The precious contents within the Holy Scriptures is not a fairy tale. The events described therein are there to help us **NOW to hold on to HOPE! Jesus is our hope.** When we hold on fervently to ***HIM who is our hope***, then we become empowered with the **WISDOM** of God found in the Scriptures to conquer the assaults on our lives. And with our grip on hope and wisdom as our armor, we then immerse ourselves in prayers to be strengthen. When we are strong especially in the Spirit, we don't fear the enemy because we know that it is God with us who makes us strong. Jesus was strong yet humble. He showed us that we should live a life inclusive of His Spirit because He promised to never leave us nor forsake us but to ask of Him for help and He will help us. He will answer us when we call.

In this book, I have shared some of the wisdom the Holy Spirit has revealed to me. It has been my continual endeavor to keep my HOPE in JESUS CHRIST. My life is one of continual prayers, trusting God and His holy words of wisdom and instructions as He helps me manage the many demands of life. In this life, surely we shall face many trials but we do not face them alone because Jesus has overcome the world and so shall we. **We have to remain in FAITH because God responds to FAITH!** We ought not to be subjected to hopelessness and the other issues we face. We are to ask the Lord to help us overcome. Journey with me through this book

"Living in Hope and Wisdom with Prayers"
Your life will be transformed from the inside out.
And now may the Lord's wisdom enfold you, as you hold on to Him as your hope refuge and strength. May the Lord speak to your heart, as you sense His divine and living presence for He desires to strengthen you and help you to overcome all the trials you will encounter. This I pray in Jesus name Amen and Amen.

Message to Readers

It is with deep reverence and respect for the Lord I approached and completed this project. It was certainly a unique journey sharing the wisdom of the Word of God. This book was conceived, carried, and written with much prayer as I birthed it. Its purpose is to guide you to live in hope and wisdom and for you to understand the importance of living a life of prayer. We are to pray about EVERYTHING. Talking to God and committing our ways to Him is a daily routine that we must practice.

The Word of God teaches us that *"we must get wisdom and guard it well"*, but I truly believe that we must also be ever prayerful as we build up hope and express our faith in God. In doing so, I believe we will lower pride and garner humility.

The messages outlined in this book are of a mixed nature. You will find some messages that are laden with detail, while others are written as *"wisdom nuggets"* or as a *"phrase page"*. I encourage you to read slowly and let your Spirit chew deliberately on the messages outlined. There is much to learn and to keep in your heart as you journey daily with the Lord.

You will also find prayers that will stir your heart, but I also encourage you to take time to pray your personal *"prayer of your heart"* to the heart of God. He loves you and loves to hear from you. Now let's begin!

Acknowledgments

The Lord is great and He is deserving of all the praise and adoration.

I give the Lord the utmost praises for the release of my fifth book! It is only by His Spirit, direction, strength and leadership I am able to accomplish this. I do not take credit nor share in His glory because I wouldn't be able to do this if He hadn't gifted me to do it. ***The Lord's Word and His Work is about Him and so I am simply His vessel to pour out His Water to His people.***

"Thank you Lord for being my everything and for loving me every day and every step of the way. I don't know where I would be in this life without you, and I am so grateful that your Hand came to rescue me, your eyes never fail from seeing me and your voice still speaks with clarity and distinction. You are excellent in all that you do and I pray that you will continue to use me to scribe your words and to do your will in Jesus name Amen"

I would also like to thank my loving and dear mother D.M. Forbes Johnson, my wonderful and kind brother H.C Johnson and my supportive and considerate son K. A. M. Gray for their love and support. You are all very instrumental in my life, encouraging me to press forth, never to quit, but to rise to the next levels until I part this earth and enter into the heavens. You all mean so very much to me and God has proved through you time and again that:

"Little is much when God is in what is being done"

Indeed the Lord still takes loaves and fish to feed the multitudes. This is what this book and my other writings will do for many. Amen.

And I shan't forget all my sisters in Christ and brothers in the Lord (you know who you are, even the new relationships that have been formed). To you I say: *"Thank You"* for being supportive and appreciative of the call that is on my life. You have been chosen to journey alongside with me and I call you my family as well. I love you all and am grateful that you are within the fabric of my life. **To my darling Mom, brother, son, and spiritual family: What I know for sure is this:** *In a dark world where someone chooses to strike a match and hold up a flame of fire, sometimes the flame may seem dim at first yet visible, but to have the right people cheering you on with their flames lighted, we corporately become a mighty blaze of fire. God has allowed us to become a mighty blaze of fire together, through the love that we have shared. It is His Light we proclaim to be the TRUTH of this world and that LIGHT can never fade. May blessings beyond measure be yours daily for His glory in Jesus name Amen!*

The Real Deal about **Abundance**

I invite you to say this phrase out loud a few times: ***"God lacks nothing! He shall supply all that I need!"***

This phrase is a catch phrase for us to remember, that our God is abundant in all that he does and there is nothing that we will ever lack if we ask of Him. God's provisions towards us will never run dry. There are people in this world who have a lack mindset even in the midst of abundance. They feel as if there isn't enough for them or they think that some people will always have more than they will. This is not true. Others may seem to have more, but you never know the real truth about their situation. We simply often see the face value of what people have and do not know the depth or truth of what is happening. Looking wealthy and being wealthy is very different.

Living in abundance is not based only on what is in a person's bank account or how much real estate a person has. Abundance is not described as how often they travel or the extent of their education. I have seen people with all of the aforementioned, living in a mansion, but dwelling in a miserable frustrated mindset combined with dilapidated health. These people will quickly trade their material wealth for peace of mind, loving healthy relationships, being able to enjoy a good laugh and a restful night of sleep.

In God's perspective, abundance is much more than having material possessions. Abundance is about having victory in life with Christ Jesus being the focal point. Abundance begins with opening our hearts and lives daily to the generous supply God wants to impart to us. We can daily receive of God's supply and measure if we only believe and choose to receive from him with expectation and joy.

There are those who question the goodness and abundance of God. They say: If God is so good and abundant, why are there so many who are suffering and poor in the world, while others are rich and seemingly prosperous but never honor God? I totally understand this type of reasoning, because at one point I did question this imbalance between poverty and exorbitant wealth.

We need to understand that God does not **cause poverty or bad things to happen to good people**. God is not the author of evil needs. Men with wicked hearts are the ones who devise wickedness against others. Sometimes curses are in effect and it will take the valiant Hand of God to help people who are stricken in desperate ways. Although God is a God of abundance, we must also realize that there are wicked and greedy people who refuse to share their wealth and abundance with others who are in need. They strategically hinder others access to resources they have been offered and oftentimes there are orchestrated systems that exclude certain groups from attaining wealth. Groups of people who have gained much abundance because of strategic systems that exclude others will eventually feel the brunt of such systems. A system that works only for a certain group and against another can only work for so long before it implodes. It is only a matter of time, because God hates injustice and no matter how long the injustice seem to prosper, it will eventually have a domino effect and will fall.

Those who steal from others to gain abundance for themselves have simply invited curses to reign upon their households and generations. They believe that storing up financial goods is a form of security but they are wrong. The only true security we have is the Lord God. God alone is the One who guarantees true long lasting abundance.

I am sure you have witnessed what occurs when people trade unfairly. This is called stealing. When unequal trade occurs for decades upon decades, the outcome is poverty for one group and lavish wealth for the clever thief. God is not mocked and God is certainly not blind. He who see injustice will deliver judgment to thieves. God has a plan and a way of turning tables by giving abundance to His people. A person may have "old money" or all sorts of investments and portfolios but true abundance and wealth comes from the True and Living God. Having a hefty portfolio but rotting in health is poverty. ***The abundance that God gives no money in the world can buy. God's portfolio is unlike the portfolio of man. Man can't buy health, love, peace, joy, and all that is in the hands and power of the Almighty God.***

God is still the God of abundance despite the evils of some. God has a way of raising up people who have a heart for the poor, to feed, clothe, educate and empower them. Because God lacks nothing and sees everything, he can even convert the heart of the wicked to do His will. God can even work in mysterious ways like that of a Robin Hood, taking from the rich to give to the poor.

God's motive is always LOVE and he shows his abundance through acts of love. When Jesus discerned that the multitudes were hungry, his heart was moved to feed them. One of his disciples Philip, went into excuse mode, stating that there wasn't enough money to purchase food to feed the 5000 present, but Andrew came with an answer. The answer was five loaves of bread and two fish. Jesus raised it up, gave thanks for it, and instructed the disciples to feed the people. All ate and still left overs remained. The point is this: God can take the little that we have and make it abundant if we have faith to believe.

Again: God lacks nothing. You must now take the initiative and see what you have to work with. Tell God that He is a miracle working God who is able to do the impossible. Have the faith to believe and honor the instructions he gives for you to do. In doing so, God will send His abundance your way.

Prayer: Father, you are the Most High God lacking nothing. Your hand is never empty and so I trust in you to supply for all my needs. You are the very expression of abundance, for you are a BIG God, enormously loving and can do grand things. I lack nothing from this day forth because I know that my God shall supply for all my needs in Jesus name Amen.

What are your **Actions** saying?

***

Here is a phrase page of wisdom and hope for you.

Be very mindful of your actions. Did you know that you are naked in your Spirit as your actions are manifested in the flesh? The demonstration of your behaviors reveals exactly what you are bearing in your Spirit. It is time to contemplate your actions and behaviors and for you to ask the Lord to bring the correction that is needed.

Heavenly Father, if my actions have not been proper nor pleasing in your sight, show me what needs correction. Lord it is through my actions and my words, my Spirit is being exposed. Lord help me to see myself in the Spirit and Lord I need you to assist me to accept the necessary corrections which will mold me to become more like you. This I pray in Jesus name Amen.

The Challenges of **Adversity**

~◆~

We will never know when we will enter into a season of adversity. During these storms of life it seems as if everything is going wrong but we can choose to keep our hope in God. Despite the tossing of life, our roots must remain strong, standing firm in Christ alone.

Jesus Christ is the Master of the storms in the spiritual as well as the natural. Jesus was once in a boat with his disciples in the midst of a squall. Jesus was asleep during the storm, however His disciples were afraid. Here we see two different perspectives. Jesus was indirectly showing them that if He was resting, they were to rest as well. Jesus wasn't afraid of the storm. He wasn't moved by the external circumstances of the waves, the rough seas or the howling wind. He was at rest. The disciples should have realized that if Jesus wasn't worried they shouldn't be worried either.

God wants us to have peace during storms of adversity. During adversity we must choose, intentionally choose to lean, depend on and cling faithfully to Jesus. We cannot depend on friends or family. We cannot depend on the money in the bank account or our jobs. All these have a level of uncertainty. People change, money can run out and positions of employment can be taken away. When we shift our focus to relying totally on God for direction, He is able to strategically direct us to the places of transformation and success. God also has a way of showing up through the people He knows has the capability to help us. During adversity, we are to pray, keep the faith, listen to God for direction, be mindful of God's blessings, resting in His Word and rejoicing prior to the breakthrough. No storm lasts forever, but those who are strong can overcome adversity. When we choose to trust God even through the storms of life, there are valuable lessons we will learn. Remember, some lessons are only learned through adversity. In addition, a certain resilience and strength is gained through adversity. Just remember to keep your hope and faith in Jesus who is always the Master of the storms.

Heavenly Father, when I am faced with the storms of adversity, help me to trust in you that you will give me the strength to lean totally on you. I will make it through if I don't let go from your Hand. You will teach me valuable lessons for the next level and I thank you for all adversities, for I will be strengthened to say that it was good that I was afflicted. You are with me Lord and just knowing that, it is enough. This I pray in Jesus name Amen.

What are you in **Agreement** with?

Here is a phrase page of wisdom and hope for you.

Who or what are you agreeing with? Be mindful about who or what you are saying yes to. Be intentional to enter into daily agreement with God instead of agreeing with the reasoning of others. This is the time to be mindful of who or what you are agreeing with. Your agreement can cause progression, regression or stagnation. Take time to think and see how your agreements are affecting your life.

Heavenly Father, I choose to come in total agreement with you and your will for my life. I set aside and put behind me everything and everyone that is not in agreement with your will for my life and future in Jesus name Amen.

Dealing with **Anger**

Here is a phrase page of wisdom and hope about dealing with anger.

Do you know someone who has a problem with controlling their temper? People who have intense problems managing their emotions can become a distraction in your life. How about you? Do you have a struggle managing yourself when angry? Getting upset and easily angered will never be the solutions to the problems we face. Too much uncontrolled anger can get us in more than we bargained for. We must learn not to be blinded by anger, but instead to seek out a solution than throw a fit. It is far better to decide to remain calm, breathe deeply, take a walk, gather ones thoughts and locate a glimpse of the solution within the problem than to let anger get loose. Ask the Lord in prayer to help you manage your emotions when angered. Ask for clarity when angered, relief from the stress of anger and how to learn value lessons when processing anger appropriately.

Lord, too often anger can cause a blockage in our thinking and focus. Help us Lord to understand the reasons for being angry, but also relieve us from the stress of it. Help us Lord to develop better strategies that are fitting to express our emotions. This we pray in Jesus name Amen.

Being Mindful of your **Associations**

Our associations, the crew we choose to be close to us, must be designed by God. Some people are very sloppy with the type of people they allow to get close to them. Did you know that there are people who strategically plant themselves in your life strictly to fulfil their purposes and their purposes only? Sometimes it is financially motivated. They want to be close to bleed you financially. Other people study your weaknesses and feed off your weaknesses to gain power over you. We cannot live an open access life. We must be intentional about closing the door on certain relationships and associations. We must open the door solely to God for Him and Him alone to bring the right associations to us, whether they be permanent, temporary or seasonal.

I need for you to understand one thing about association: We tend to learn habits, whether good or evil from those we associate with. Habits are easily formed, but at times are extremely difficult to end. Choose wisely your associations. Should God show you whom to cut loose, cut them loose! If God shows you that an association will bring meaning, blessings, purpose and glory to God then hold on to it until God speaks otherwise. Never be afraid to disrobe yourself from an association and move on to who, what and where He leads.

Lord, you were very mindful of choosing the people to be with you in ministry. My life is a ministry and therefore I need to be mindful of who I associate with. Associations can bless me or stress me, so help me Lord to accept who you have sent and let go of who needs to go in Jesus name Amen.

Believing *in Yourself*

Have you ever struggled with believing in yourself? Yes, I have had those days until the revelation dawned on me like the noon day sun that I am not a random act of God. I know that God has created me for a purpose and as a bird was made to sing, I must BECOME whom GOD has called me to become without feeling guilty. God has endowed us with His talents and abilities, therefore we must bring Him glory by using the gifts for His kingdom purposes. Amen.

Let today be the day you understand how unique and awesomely wonderful you are. I have gained joy watching others moving effortlessly in their gifting and abilities. Did you know that we were built for life? Yes! God has created you and me for a purpose and that purpose is this: **To Do His Will**. Yes, I am created to do His will and yes that is exactly what I am doing. How about you?

Think about the various animals and species on this earth. A fish, a bird, a horse, a tree, a plant, a bacteria, a mouse, a dog, a butterfly and more are all doing exactly what they have been created to do. Even evil is doing its purpose, therefore why should we not do what we are built to do? We must believe the God who created us and speak to thyself and say:

"I believe you God so I believe in me."

Let today be the day you stop lying to yourself that you cant. You can do all that God has created you to do. Work diligently towards what God wants you to accomplish. Believe God. Believe in yourself.

Heavenly Father you have created me with abilities that are unique and wonderful. I am a gift to this world, having the qualities that the world needs at this time. Help me Lord to stop doubting myself. Help me Lord to believe that I can use these abilities to serve you and mankind. Remove the blindfolds off my mind, eyes and heart and give me a new vision of myself with courage and strong faith to accomplish my purpose in Jesus name Amen.

Overcoming a **Broken Heart**

❧❖❧

I am familiar with the pain of a broken heart. It is not the easiest thing to endure, but with the proper amount of time and Godly intervention, a person can come out stronger from a broken heart.

I have learned that when we give our hearts to people who are careless, immature and selfish, they will indeed toy with the treasures of love contained therein. After their play time with our precious love is over, a shattered heart remains and at times a shattered spirit and mind may be the end result.

Those with a broken heart tend to end up being bitter and hopeless about loving again. Others end up in depression or battle with anger spells. Many commit suicide because of the trespass of trust/love while others resort to retaliation.

Jesus was very familiar with those with a broken heart. The heart of God was first broken when his most prized possession, his children, got separated from a loving intimate relationship with Him. Jesus is our bridge back to wholeness from a broken heart.

Jesus understands the venom of deceit. He knows what it feels like to be rejected and unloved. He also knows that there are no self-help remedies that can help those with a broken heart. He desires that we choose to come to Him for guidance, direction and the true spiritual intervention needed for a broken heart. Spiritual issues of the heart need spiritual intervention, and because Jesus created hearts he knows how to heal broken hearts. The Lord is able to expunge spiritual shatter and wounds of the heart. Ask God in the hush of utter silence to slowly and tenderly remove all poisons, all wounds, all bitterness and all damages of a broken heart.

Heavenly Father I ask you Lord to heal my broken heart. You know the wounds within. You know the disappointments. You know what has infected and affected my heart when I loved and trusted others. Only your remedy can cure all deep pains in my heart, so I ask that you heal my heart Lord and it will be healed. In Jesus name Amen

*Answering the **Call** on Your Life*

You are not a mistake. Your life is not by chance and you have been created and called for a purpose. Many in this world do not embrace the fact that they have been created by God for a purpose. God does not make mistakes or does things randomly without reason.

God intentionally thought about you and your life before you came into being. Think about it. As a fish, a dog, a horse, a plant, a shrimp and the minute cells in your body has purpose, you too my friend, have purpose breathing in your being. Not only do you have purpose, but God strategically and specifically calls some people to do His work! You could be one!

Our lives are in essence not our own, but created to be used by God. We may fight *"the call"* all we want, but will only feel frustrated and misaligned if we aren't in the correct setting that God designed for us. It is always best to surrender to the call.

This call is a mission oriented one to help those who need the gift, talent and abilities we hold. Your life is actually an answer, a solution to some problem. We see this with people who were determined to create the solutions to different problems. The traffic signal, a computer, a light bulb, a broom, etc. were all birth out of a need. There was a problem present in the world and someone discovered the solution to the problem. That person was created by God at that specific time in history to solve that problem. We all are teeming with ideas and solutions to problems. Your life is needed to solve a problem not to create one.

Will you surrender to God and answer the call? Will you walk into your destiny and purpose so that you can make a difference in this world? It doesn't matter how grand the purpose may be, just understand that it matters and you are needed. Every life matters on this earth. Simply trust the Master's plan and be led by the Lord each day as you move closer to your destiny.

When Jesus called the disciples, they didn't understand the full measure of the call. They walked with Jesus and witnessed the miracles and the impact that was being made in the lives of people all about. When Jesus died, rose from the dead and ascended into Heaven, it was their time to walk into their destiny. And they did. God will not usher us into our divine destiny unless He has prepared us to do what is needed. We should simply follow His lead. His leadership can be trusted so trust Him and be about your Father's business.

Heavenly Father, thank you that you created me for a purpose. This purpose has a specified call that I need to accomplish on this earth. Help me to follow your lead and to do exactly what you want me to do.

I am not my own and I need to focus on being about my Father's business. Strengthen and prepare me when I don't know it all, but I can rest in trusting your leadership. This I pray in Jesus name Amen.

Making **Choices**

⚜

Choices, choices, choices. We are flooded to make choices each and every day of our lives. Some choices are easier to make than others, but they still need to be made. Jesus had to make choices as well and one of the biggest choices he made was to lay down His life to be sacrificed for the redemption of our own. What a choice! Jesus knew we were more than worth it. I am grateful He did choose me, so that I can have an intimate relationship with Him to know the eternal promises of the Kingdom of God. I am satisfied that my life will not end in torment, but in eternal life with the King of kings and Lord of lords. Amen.

How about you? What are some of the choices you are making? Your choices today affect your tomorrows. Yes. Where you are at currently in your life is due to a choice you made in your yesterdays. Don't blame anyone for any mishap in your life. Yes, there are some unfortunate happenings that occur in our lives, but we can chose to rise up from those mishaps by changing our mindset. What happened happened, and it cannot be changed. Being stuck in your head by what occurred five years ago will not help you today. You can choose to move forward, backward, upward, downward or get stuck in the head! Will you choose to move on today?

The disciple Peter, denied he knew Jesus in the middle of Jesus' greatest spiritual battles of judgment. Peter was recognized that he belonged to those who were constantly with Jesus, but because of fear, Peter chose to cover his identity of being a disciple of Jesus. Peter later became grieved in His spirit when what Jesus prophesied about the rooster crowing after Peter's several denials came through. Peter wept bitterly because he felt as if he did the unthinkable.

We too at times have had those unthinkable moments and circumstances in life that grieved us. Sometimes we rehearse the hurt and find it difficult to choose to forgive ourselves. Due to bad choices, many go into hiding because of remorse, but Jesus wants us to move forward from our failures.

I have made some really bad choices in life, but the Lord had to show me that He is my Redeemer and Restorer from bad choices. ***Once we are alive, we can choose to re-choose***. One of the best choices I recommend to people is to choose Jesus to be Lord of their choices. I encourage you now to choose Jesus to be Lord of your life, for He will lead you into the correct paths of righteousness and blessings. If you haven't chosen Jesus, and have chosen everything else in the past but Him, will you choose Jesus today? If you do, undoubtedly, it will be one of the BEST choices you will ever make in your life. Amen.

My Heavenly Father, I thank you for choosing me to have eternal life by the sacrificial work of dying a gruesome death on a cross for my sins. Lord, now I am at a junction where I want to choose you because everything else I have chosen didn't work out too well for me. Come into my heart. Forgive me of my sins. I am choosing you to be Lord over my life in Jesus name Amen.

Dealing with **Competition**

Allow me to get a bit transparent. This word, competition, is not my favorite word. Now, it's not because I like or dislike competition. It is because I have seen how some people behave obnoxiously during a competition that irks me. I often stay away from competition because I really don't think that competitions are a fare way of assessing a person's strengths or abilities. I often don't agree with the main aim of competing nor see the worth of competing valuable because each person is different and have their own specific skillsets.

I have learned that some people entered in a secret competition with you that you knew nothing about. Their intentions were to prove something to you or to try to outshine you on a project or in life in. The Spirit of competition has its place, however if competing causes unnecessary stress, then it is always best to be your own competitor rather than try to compare yourself or your skills with another.

We observe the spirit of competition all around us. We see banks compete for customers. Credit card companies try to offer rates that are better than their competitors. Different programs compete for business. Fashion designers compete for recognition. Employees compete for positions and so forth. The aim of competition is to gain the envied number one position. Know this for sure: Being number one doesn't always mean that you are the best. Being number one today doesn't mean being number one forever. There will always be someone who will come along and break the record and outshine yesterday's glory.

A person who understand who they are, need not try to compete with others. They run their own race, knowing that their gift and talents will make room for them and they are satisfied in their calling. God has created all of us to be genius in something specific that is unique and different from the rest. We simply need to be the best in our mind and leave the stress of competition at the door.

We can learn so much from the animal kingdom. I love lions, tigers and cats. In my opinion, they are confident and calm creatures when needs be, and fiercely brutal when necessary. They know what they are about, go after what they want, rest when they must, hunt as needed, defend and protect when necessary. Lions in particular give a mighty roar to prove its dominance and presence. They don't compete. They simply fight and gain what they want.

Some people who aren't confident in whom they are feel the need to be in competition with others. I love how Jesus taught in parables, fed the people and was about His Father's business healing and delivering those who were oppressed. Although the Pharisees and Sadducees were amazed at his authority and teachings, I believe that they were jealous as well. This didn't stop Jesus from doing what He was called and created to do. The Pharisees were in a secret competition with Jesus always questioning Him and seeking to destroy and disgrace the King of Glory. But Jesus knew beforehand their schemes and didn't get side tracked by their interruptions. He used those opportunities to teach them about the kingdom and about the condition of their hearts.

At times competition can be fun. We can learn a lot about the condition of our heart and the true motivations behind competitions. Are we trying to prove something to others when competing or are we trying to become better at what we do? It ought to be our aim to shine forth the unique and intrinsic qualities to the glory of God. We are to marvel at the awesome work that God does through another vessel rather than hinder, be jealous of, be negative about or compete with it. God sees our heart and knows that an inappropriate competitive spirit will get us nowhere.

And remember, no one in this world is 100% perfect. When we choose to put our gifts and abilities together to reach a goal, rather than compete, we can get more accomplished to show forth the power and creativity of our Almighty God through us, His best creation!

Heavenly Father, your Word declares that we are fearfully and wonderfully made. You created us to show forth the wonder of your glory, not to compete with others. Lord, remove any inappropriate competitive spirit within us and help us to be satisfied with the gifts and abilities you have bestowed upon us. My life is to bring you glory and not to compete with others. This I pray in Jesus name Amen.

Giving God **Control**

I will never forget an incident I had with my mother and how God used my brother to help me to handle it. My mother had her mindset on having a particular procedure done and I was all against it. I had done research on it, heard about certain outcomes and shared the information with her. I prayed with her about it but she went ahead and did the procedure anyway. I wasn't too happy. In my response, I decided to speak to my brother about it who calmly reminded me to simply stop stressing myself out, pray continually, keep the faith, leave it in God's hands for God can take care of it. He reminded me that if Mom chose not to listen it was not in my control but God's. Now this was a simple enough explanation, but for some reason those last words he said: "It is not in my control but God's" catapulted me to a new dimension.

How about you? Have you been stressing yourself over things that you simply don't have control over? It could be aging parents, troublesome children, financial issues, family situations, job related complications, health ailments etc. that are wrecking your nerves and patience. You want it under control now but everything you try seem to work against your efforts. ***The point we ought to remember is this: We are not in control.*** We weren't in control of our birth, neither are we in control over the day we die. We are not even in control of our hearts beating, our breathing or the blood circulating through our bodies. There are many decisions and things in operation that are clearly out of our control because it is God who is in control of specific happenings. Yes, we do have to make choices but the outcomes and consequences are in God's hand to issue.

My son and I had a discussion about whether we have control over our lives from life to death. He chose to point out to me that people who commit suicide chose to end their lives on a particular day. Even so, I know someone who did attempt to kill herself but she was later found and spared. In that case, she wanted to die, but God sovereignly purposed that her life would be saved. Not every suicide attempt came out like this, but I believe that God knows the very date that we must leave this earth and it is his word that has the final say.

For me, I choose to surrender certain circumstances into the powerful hands of God. When I do, I experience more peace. This is especially effective when you deal with stubborn people. You may try to help them but they will refuse your help. Never get offended, just let it go. Letting go to let God have ultimate control is not the easiest thing to do, but it is oftentimes necessary. We must learn to lean on God when things seem as if it is spiraling out of control. Once it is in God's hands, consider it safe.

I remember a biblical event with the woman who had the issue of blood. She was at her wits end. She was at the end of her road with money, dealing with constant vaginal bleeding and she just had enough. She chose to use her hand as a point of contact to touch the hem of Jesus' garment, signaling that she had tried everything. Her hands were bare with no money left, tired of bleeding and so she gave her problem to God. I can hear her saying in her mind: ***"I let it go Jesus. I let it go and give it to you as I touch the hem of your garment by faith."*** Her faith of letting go and touching the hem of the Healer's garment did make her whole for she decided she couldn't handle it, but she knew Jesus could. This woman realized that her attempts of being in control wasn't getting her results, and so she decided to put God in control and she got results. Now her results may not be similar to your results when you decide to let go, but know for sure that when God is in control, the outcome will be way better and well worth it. Learn to lean on God and surrender control to God. In His hands circumstances are safe for He can handle it all!

Lord, when I want to be in control, remind me, teach me and help me to trust you that you have my best interest at heart. Help me to feel at ease with surrendering circumstances into your care for you care for me. When you are in control, I will see the outcome that is best for all involved. This I pray in Jesus name Amen.

Dealing with **Delay** *and* **Denial**

Have you ever wondered why when you pray, it seems as if the answer to your prayers will never be answered or you doubt God heard your prayers? I know firsthand what it feels like to wait, and wait and wait and wait some more! Waiting is certainly a test of patience. I have learned that patience is something very good to master even when it means being delayed or being denied.

There are some delays that are completely frustrating and are purposed by the enemy of our soul. You see, God has particular works that we must accomplish for his purposes on the earth realm. The enemy of our soul seeks to impede the work of God. There will always be a fight between what God wants to accomplish in and through us and what the enemy wants to do. We must be very mindful about this battle that exists. For example: We must be mindful of what we are doing with our precious time. Too often, we spend time doing things that are worthless and do not bring meaning nor fullness to the potential within us. When our time is consumed doing nonsense then we become ineffective. The more time we waste on the wrong things is the less time we have on our side to accomplish the right things. Wasted time consumes our time to manifest our destiny.

God is the God of movement. His movement is always forward and not backward. He is eternal and not fixed to the limitations of time for He created time. In the book of Ecclesiastes, it states: ***"There is a time and season for everything under the heavens."***

There are certain times and seasons for things to be accomplished in our lives. The spirit of delay messes with the order of things in our lives. ***Learn this truth: satan is the one who wants to delay, stagnate and deny us of what God has timely purposed for us.*** The more time we waste, the more blessings we end up forfeiting. Satan is a thief! He uses the spirit of laziness, procrastination, doubt, excuses and all he can think of to delay us. We should be in tuned with the mouth of God and as He speaks to us we are to go forth and do! Why? The thief cometh not but to kill, steal and destroy the very word God has spoken to us. Do not give him the chance to take your blessings away.

Let this be the day you look in retrospect at your life and identify the patterns of delay that you accepted. Seek God and prayerfully ask for forgiveness for accepting the lies and misdeeds of your flesh, such as procrastination and fear. Ask God to build you up to act on His word with diligence and drive.

Heavenly Father, I come boldly asking you to intercept the plans and strategies of the enemy seeking to delay and deny me of my rightful place and blessings. Help me to choose your Word and instructions above all else. Help me to be obedient and act faithfully to accomplish my purpose within the times and seasons you have set. This I pray in Jesus name Amen

Depending *on God*

I am sure you know someone who is a needy person. Their need is so great it can be quite draining and at times you don't want to be around that person for long. How about you? Do you consider yourself a needy person? You always have the need to be around people or you need something from someone? Be honest with yourself because in order to gain freedom, one must first look within to see if there are any fractures or wounds.

So let me say this as simply as possible: *We all need God so we all need to depend on God first and foremost.* Many people will not embrace this saying at first, but tough experiences will encourage some people to. God has a way of showing us that there is no person on this planet who can fill our every need. When we give God full reign to design our relationships we will be better off. A friend did share with me that if we choose to first love freely and choose to please God by pleasing others, then relationships will be more successful. When people aim to please each other and love is reciprocated, then there will be more satisfaction in relationships. I agree with this concept, because people will be focused on pleasing rather than being pleased.

Our Heavenly Father sent his Son Jesus to show us that we can trust Him all the way. We can totally depend on God and not be disappointed. Why? God knows it all about us. Even the things we don't quite yet know about ourselves He knows. He created us and knows what will make us happy, what will disappoint us, what will send us crazy, what we will love, what we will enjoy, what will bring us grief, what will make us laugh, what will anger us and so much more. It should be a breeze to surrender our lives to the One who created us because every facet of our being He already knows about.

Jesus once met a woman at a well at midday as she was drawing water from it. He sparked a conversation with her. He asked her for a drink. But what Jesus was really aiming for was what was occurring in her life. He saw that not only was she drawing for physical water to satisfy her physical thirst, but her soul was thirsty for Living Waters. Jesus was able to reveal to her that she had five husbands and the one she was living with wasn't her husband. Oh boy! Talk about Jesus up in your business! Can you imagine what this woman was thinking in her head: ***"Who is this man? I don't know him so how is it he knows my business like this?"*** Oh yes, Jesus knew her because He knew her before she was born and He had His eye on her up to that very point. He knew that she was trying to get her thirst filled from these "husbands". These men couldn't quench her inner thirst. She was depending on them when she should have been depending on God. Isn't that what some of us still do? I will be the first one to confess that there were times I depended on people rather than depend on the ONE who is DEPENDABLE.

It is always best to depend on God. People will leave you, die, turn their backs, curse you out and leave you stranded but God will never leave us nor forsake us because He loves us too much to do so.

Heavenly Father, help me to shift my mindset from depending on people to total dependency on You the True and Living God. You are all that I need for you are the MORE THAN ENOUGH. Your hands are never too short to save and never empty to give. You said you will provide for all that I need for you care about me. Thank you that I can call you Father and your heart is for me and never against me. I now rest in you and your abundance that daily flows my way and loads me up with favor and benefits this day and always in Jesus name Amen.

Dealing with **Discouragement**

At some point of our lives we will experience some sort of discouragement and hopelessness. Indeed, discouragement can become extreme where we feel like we want to snap like a tree branch being bent too far. God does not desire for us to break apart. He wants us to bounce back from all sorts of issues and become stronger than before.

Yes, the stressors in life are real, but we cannot allow them to get the best of us. We must learn how to make the necessary adjustments to be resilient. The Word of God tells us to ***"be strong in the Lord and in the power of the Lord's might"***. This verse makes me think about the Lord Jesus being on the cross during His gruesome crucifixion. At one point Jesus said: ***"Eloi Eloi lama sabachthani"*** which translates as ***"Father, Father, why have you forsaken me?"*** At that point of Jesus' wail to the Heavenly Father, Jesus had the sins of the entire world and I believe that cry was a cry of discouragement. The human side of Jesus was feeling the weight of the world and so could have felt alone, burdened and separated from His Heavenly Father God. Have you ever had a crucifixion moment? Where you felt like you had so much on your shoulders, bearing the weight of responsibilities, feeling alone without anyone to help you? If yes, then Jesus understood it too. Jesus was so used to having the presence of Father God with Him, that not sensing His presence was a bit too much for the human side of him to bear.

It's not that God leaves us or forsakes us. God did say that He would never leave us nor forsake us and the Lord is true to His word. But God will look and see how we respond and manage the weight of what we carry. For Jesus, the Son of God, He cried out to the Father in his time of discouragement. How are you responding to discouragements? How are you managing what you feel in times of discouragements and hopelessness? Do you cry out to God as Jesus did or are you cussing, drinking, drugging and falling back into habits rather than depending on God?

We all have a breaking point and what we go through can either break us, sink us or helps us to lean on and depend on God more. God never meant for us to do life alone. Many people choose to handle it "solo" but in reality, we were designed to depend on God. God is always a very present help in times of trouble and this includes times of discouragement. We are to rest in His care. When we truly surrender to God and put Him first in all things, the Lord in turn is free to do what He desires for us, in us and through us. Surrender means to pray and ask God for His help in times when we feel discouraged and hopeless. And as

David did, we also should do which is to **"encourage thyself in the Word of God."** Speak to your soul words of life and look to the Lord who will lift up your soul.

Heavenly Father, in times when I feel discouraged and hopeless, help me to surrender totally to you for help. Help me to be more prayerful, feeding on your Word and praising your name, because in doing so, you will restore joy which will break the pain of discouragement. You are my help and I will continually depend on you in Jesus name Amen.

What You Need to Know About **Evil**

As children of the Most High God, we will encounter many evils that try to intimidate us. Know this for sure: When we live a holy life unto the Lord, keeping the lines of communication open with Him and obeying His directives, the evil that seeks to come against us will not have any power over us. It is written that ***"no weapon formed against us shall prosper and every tongue that rises against us the Lord shall condemn it!"*** Indeed, this Scripture lets us know that weapons will form, but they shall NOT prosper. Neither will tongues that speak evil against us prevail, because the Lord who made tongues can shut up mouths. We who have tongues have the power to speak life over ourselves and shut down the negative words that seek to speak evil against us.

I remember an incident that occurred in a work environment years ago. This woman had a serious issue with me from the first day I started the job. Her eyes of hatred spoke all it had to say when she glared at me. I realized what I was dealing with and so I deliberately decided not to give her fuel for her fire. I loved on her and was pleasant to her, but she was quietly angered by my very presence. One day I noticed how she handled a particular person and it bothered me so I prayed in my heart as the Lord led me to as I worked in her presence. She tried really hard to get me to retaliate and be disrespectful to her as she spewed a range of evil words my way in the presence of officials, pointing her fingers like claws toward me, claiming that my time to lose my job was next. I pointed right back to her and said: ***"Your words have no power over me and I cancel your words against me and they are returned to you in Jesus name."*** In a month she lost her job. Apparently this woman was a problem for many years. She was probably battling with many things and needed help but she refused. Evil in essence took hold of her heart, mind and life trying to use her as a tool to torment others, but that day I was not having that.

We must know for sure that evil principalities, powers and rulers are under the subjection of the powerful Almighty Hand of God and Jesus showed us that demons flee at the name, authority and presence of **JESUS**.

We need not fear evil for evil first fears us. It wants us to think otherwise that it has more power but it is JESUS who has the true power. And we have been given the power to place evil in its place which is under our feet because Jesus stepped on and crushed the head of the enemy. Evil cannot conquer the power of love because LOVE conquers ALL. This is not implying to love evil. Evil is evil and there is nothing within it to love. God does however wants us to pray for those who are blinded, thinking that evil is good. People who are involved in activities such as witchcrafts, wizardry, obeah, necromancy etc. are being fooled by satan. Praying for them is the best thing you can do to help them so that the truth will eventually be revealed to them that Jesus holds the true and absolute power in this entire universe.

Heavenly Father, I am so glad that I am untouched by my enemies. The evils that exist in this world are nothing compared to the power in your Almighty Hands. Lord, you said that you will not allow the enemies of our soul to have their way with us and for that we are grateful. We place all types of evils including witchcrafts, wizardry, obeah, necromancy and all satanic methods and practices under our feet, because they are all under the footstool of Christ Jesus. We place you O Lord Jesus in the highest place as Lord and Savior of our entire life. We respect you Lord for cancelling all the designs of the enemy against us. Lord we ask that you keep on keeping us in Your Heavenly safety, the arms of Jesus Christ. This we pray and believe in Jesus name Amen.

Do You Often Feel **Excluded**?

～✦～

Here is a nugget of wisdom and hope about being excluded.

Know for sure that when you are being excluded, don't let it get you down. God has a way of strategically excluding his children from certain activities, events, people, information and locations. Exclusion is often a blessing and a benefit that brings glory to the King of kings and Lord of lords. God has designed some people for His use only and not for the whoring of the world.

Heavenly Father, thank you for the times you purposely excluded me from certain people, places, activities, events and information. Help me to recognize that often you are trying to protect me from harm and even granting me blessings that I know not of as yet. Help me to be grateful that divine exclusion also means divine inclusion for your purposes and for your glory. This I pray in Jesus name Amen.

Living by **Faith**

Allow me to share an experience I had at a train station. I was heading to get some errands done and I needed to do it as quickly as possible. I decided to hop on the train. When I got to the train station the information dashboard reported that the next train wouldn't come for the next 15 minutes. This was not good because I had other things to get done within a certain amount of time. Seeing that I had no control of the train I whispered a prayer and decided to sit upstairs and wait until the information changed. The Holy Spirit instructed me and said: ***"Go downstairs."*** To be honest, I didn't want to go downstairs because the information stated that the next train wouldn't be there until 15minutes. Nevertheless, I went downstairs.

On getting downstairs, I was surprised and happy to see a train waiting there. I hadn't heard the engine or its presence upstairs and wondered why the information board had read differently. Within a minute of entering the train, it pulled off. Can you imagine my elation? The point that I want to share is a valuable lesson. It's this: ***Faith and Obedience hold each other's hands as they move forward.***

Although I prayed in faith, if I hadn't listened and obeyed the voice of God, I would have missed the train. Despite what the message board said, I acted by faith and obeyed the voice of God and went downstairs to be greeted by a lovely surprise: an already existing train that took me to my destination. You see, faith is not what we already see. Faith is believing God to present and work things out in His timing, despite what it looks like in the natural (in this case, the message board which stated that the next train would have been there the next 15 minutes) We cannot look at circumstances in the natural and allow what we see to quench our faith. Faith is seeing with spiritual eyes and believing in our hearts that God is capable of doing what we have asked of him and even more. God has a way of giving us greater than what we expected. Never underestimate the power of God. There is nothing impossible for God to do, however, we should be open to accepting what God does, rather than seeking to figure out how God will do what we have asked.

Remember: Faith speaks the possible not the impossible. Faith speaks the positives not the negatives. Faith utters what it wants, not what it fears. Faith communicates answers and solutions not problems and issues. Faith uplifts and transforms not burdens and deforms. Let us rise up and live by faith not in fear.

Heavenly Father, you want us to live by faith, for it is faith that pleases you the most. Expunge and destroy all spirits of fear that limits us and help us to sharpen our faith by obeying you and your Word. We ask that you increase our faith and dependence on you, for there is nothing too hard or impossible for you to do. Help us to see with the eyes of faith and to believe with a heart of faith. Remove the scales of fear and help us to know that because you are faithful we can put our faith in you in Jesus name we pray Amen.

How to **Flow**

Jesus managed his earthly ministry by allowing God to flow in and through Him. There is something so beautiful about flowing in the Spirit of God, that we should all desire this for our lives. God wants to use us as His vessels to flow through. Jesus came to do the will of the Father and that meant to be surrendered to God totally.

God has a heavenly will that needs to be accomplished on the earth realm. It is impossible to allow God to flow through us and want to do our own thing at the same time. I remember an incident that taught me a valuable lesson about flow. It was a rainy morning and I was heading to work. It was also very windy and I struggled to manage the umbrella because the rain and wind was blowing in the opposite direction to where I desired to go. This was certainly a test in resistance. As I struggled to keep the umbrella up, I decided to let the wind and rain win, rather than to press forward in a fight with it, seeing that my hands were tired, garments wet and attitude annoyed. When I allowed the wind to carry me in the direction it wanted, I had no resistance from it. I was simply flowing with the wind. I didn't even have to put much effort in because the flow of the wind was pushing me to move in the direction it wanted. Of course, I had to go to work, so I waited until the wind died down.

This example of the flow of the wind is similar to what God wants us to do as a surrender to His flow. We will face much opposition, annoyance, exhaustion, energy output and even unnecessary expense, when we try to do things our way rather than God's way. We simply need to allow God to have open access to flow in and through our lives. When we do surrender to God's flow, God will bless us and use us as a conduit to impact lives on earth and effect change in environments.

Heavenly Father, I surrender my ways for your ways. Have your way with my heart, mind, Spirit and soul so that you can flow through me and glory will come to you. You have prepared a work for me to do and therefore I give you my all. Flow Lord Jesus. Flow through me for your glory and the good of mankind in Jesus name I pray Amen.

Focus! Focus! **Focus!**

Undeniably, we live in a busy and hectic world and at times it is difficult to keep our focus. The many offerings that vie for our attention on a minute by minute basis, seem more than the hair on our heads, but we must be strong and determined to maintain our focus on the people and things that matter the most.

In order to maintain focus, our objectives and goals must be clear. Additionally, we have to block out times within each day to work on the things that are important. This means we must shut the door, shut off the phones, computers and everything that seeks to distract us. This takes a lot of discipline to do and we must ask for help when needs be. If we aren't selective with what we do with our time, then chances are we become *slaves to time and not master of it.* Saying "no" to time eaters must be a part of your daily routine.

Whenever you have chosen to accomplish a goal or a task, distractors and all types of distractions come running begging for your attention. You have the power to say *"no"* to them because you have the right to your time. You need not be rude to stealers of time, but you can be straight forward, simply letting them know that you are unavailable without expressing reasons. Your time is yours, not theirs. Our lives are not designed the same.

I enjoy reading how Jesus managed his life, relationships, time and ministry. Jesus truly was focused and about his Father's business. Whenever he ministered, he was focused on specific assignments that were in alignment with his purpose. He often took time to pray to His Father and He was intentional when He chose his disciples and how he taught them. Jesus was mission minded and not randomly living his life. Jesus had specified times he prayed, slept, rested, travelled and fellowshipped.

Living a purposeful and intentional life with focus is very powerful. However, be mindful that not all distractions are bad. Some distractions warrant our attention and we must heed to them because sometimes God intercepts our focus to help us along our way. Sometimes we need a pause from focus so that we do what God wants to add and then we can return to focusing on the goals.

When we face distractions that seek to weary and weaken us, rather than help us win, we must learn to wean them off. Today, let our focus be at the bulls eye, ignoring unwarranted distractions so that we can accomplish our goals.

Heavenly Father as Jesus was focused on His goals, help me to be focused on accomplishing what you have designed for me to do on the earth realm for your glory. Help me to manage my time wisely and efficiently, weaning off distractors and identifying all your divine interruptions, so that I can add what you have revealed. This I pray in Jesus name Amen.

Godly **Friendships**

Here is a nugget of wisdom and hope about Godly friendships.

Allow the Lord to build your friendships. He has a way of bringing people together to accomplish His purposes. When we allow God to build friendships, we realize that they are more relevant and revitalizing in our lives. We don't have to "beg for" or "buy into" friendships. Neither do we have to hold on to people who are hurting us. What God does He does it well and we are to trust Him when friendships come to a close. And most of all, enjoy the friendships that God designs and establishes in your life, for it is a blessing to have the right people who will remain with us despite the seasons we face in life.

Heavenly Father, you call us FRIEND and certainly you desire that I have righteous friendships that have purpose and meaning. Establish them in my life O Lord so that glory and honor will be given to your holy name in Jesus name Amen.

Dealing with **Grief**

We will all experience some type of grief in our lives. Whether it be the loss of a loved one, a family issue that grieves your heart, a betrayal, some sort of sabotage on the job or a grueling problem, grief is something we will have to learn to process and deal with.

Dealing with the loss of a loved one is never easy, but we can also choose how to deal with the loss. We all have the power to choose. We can allow the sadness to overtake us or we can choose to accept that there is a time and season for everyone who has a lifespan. Letting go and saying goodbye to people you have had deep bonds with, is not easy, but it is a part of life and it is necessary to say goodbye. We must learn to give the gift of goodbye both in life and in death.

Grief is not necessarily a bad thing. We can learn much about ourselves and others during the process. I remember when my dad died. It was quite unexpected and I thought it would have shattered my world. I cried endlessly at the emptiness I felt in my heart and I couldn't bear the cloak of grief. I decided one day that I had to rise up out of it. I took the stance that my days of mourning his loss came to an end and I turned my mind away from missing hearing his voice, to choosing to recall his loving heart towards me. I chose to look at his pictures, remember his jokes and look within myself and see much of him within me. It was my time to carry on a piece of his brilliance, mixed in with my unique brilliance.

We all can gain a new perspective and experience a portion of growth and development through the grieving process. This occurred with my dad, but when my cousin Ofiji passed away, God allowed me to experience a new dimension of grief. Although my cousin battled with a certain illness for most of his life, I was determined that God could heal him through prayers. This was my deliberate hope believing God's best for him. When he died I was stressed, confused and disappointed. I laid on my couch and I cried. I didn't answer the phone and I cried. I had no appetite and I cried. I cried a million tears or more asking God why he didn't heal him.

But through the process God showed me that Ofiji's time on earth came to an end and it was time for all those whom lives he impacted to bid him farewell. He had finished the race and it was time for him to gain his crown and rest in peace. You see, Ofiji made an indelible mark on the lives of people around the globe. He battled fiercely with the illness, but he didn't live a limited life. He didn't allow the illness to define him or stop him from pursuing his purpose and even gaining a doctoral degree. He travelled extensively when he was often warned not to travel. But most of all, he loved and served God with all his heart. He made a difference while he was alive.

During the grieving process, I learned that we ought to rejoice especially when the righteous man or woman dies in Christ, because they are better off than the living. They are at peace, a far greater and better peace than this world can ever give.

The pain and hollowness of grief can be touched by the heart and hand of God to bring healing and comfort. Despite what grieves you, ask the Lord to teach you the lessons you can learn through the process and ask Him to bring healing and comfort to your hurting heart. Amen.

Heavenly Father, Jesus grieves when we grieve and we know that you are aware of the sadness in our hearts. You understand loss and you identify with our griefs. We know that you have the ability to heal hurting hearts and we ask that you fill up the emptiness we experience because of grief and remove the pain of sadness. Comfort our souls Lord. We thank you in advance that you will give us the strength to rejoice and move forward from the spirit of grief and heaviness. This we pray in Jesus name Amen.

Maintaining Your **Health**

Being ill and suffering from decreased health can be a horror within itself. Overcoming maladies in the mind, body and spirit can be an intense struggle, but know for sure that God is able and willing to help us even when ill.

It was never God's plan for human beings to suffer sickness. Some people have been fooled into thinking that sickness is part of their portion. ***Know this for sure: Jesus never got sick. He healed the sick.*** The bible also states that God desires that we prosper and be in **GOOD HEALTH**. Did you hear that? Good health is what God desires for you and for me and because God said it, we should believe it.

So, you may have been sick for many years, even since birth. You may believe that you will never get well, but the truth is Jesus is a Healer and he even healed those who were blind and lame from birth. He has the ability to perform a miracle in your life and shift your life from illness to wellness. ***There is nothing too hard for God to do, but we must always leave the outcome in the Father's hands.***

I moved from a place of sickness to a place of health and wellness, but there is much work that needs to be done. To regain one's health, that person must understand that it may not be an overnight process to wellness. Certain processes may be tailored made for you, but you need to stick to the process to get results. Processes may include: changing your eating habits, monitoring what or who stresses you out, exercising more, balancing your work leisure life, etc. Many sicknesses are spiritually rooted and need to be dealt with in the realm of the spirit. Did you know that a wounded spirit can manifest as a sickness in the body? Yes. I believe that certain illnesses such as depression, anxiety disorders etc. are spiritual wounds. Wounds that inflict a person on a psychological level need to be addressed within a certain period of time. Wounds that don't heal lodge in the mind of the person and manifest through the behaviors and symptoms of the disorder.

One of the first paths to take to be healed from psychological wounds is to renew our minds. We have the power to change our minds as it relates to sickness and wellness. If you already think that you will never be well, then you are already defeated. But if you think that you can overcome an illness, you have faith to regain health.

Let me encourage you that God cares about our health. Sickness sucks the life out of people and God is not happy to see his children suffering. God cares about us since the very beginning. He made sure He gave us the first food guide in the book of Genesis. God desires us to eat the right foods such as vegetables and fruits seeing that he designed our bodies in a delicate way. He knows exactly what is appropriate for us to consume. A delicate body should not be consuming harsh substances. Think about it like this: If you pour acid on a delicate fabric like lace, it will tear down to nothing. Be very selective about what you consume.

Consumption also includes spiritual things. It is the spirit of a man that sustains a man in sickness or in health. Be mindful of consuming spiritual junk in your ear, eye and mind gates. We should allow ourselves to receive faith substances which are the things of God. We should learn to reject fear based information. Think about how you feel when you are afraid. Your heart races. Your breathing alters. You feel nervous and your cognitive processes change from peace to confusion. When we constantly live fear based it has a negative impact on our health. We are to live faith based and reject the lies of the evil one. God loves us and wants us to trust him and not the lies of the evil one.

In addition, we need to be mindful of the thoughts we entertain and the places we go. If you are not in control of your mind, it will tell your feet where to go. Jesus was mindful of where he went and who he was around. We should not allow ourselves to be led by our feelings or be led by people into active graveyards. There are negative influences in these places that seek to attach to your mind and your heart. If you are around drug users or people who eat unhealthily often enough, then chances are their influence will eventually influence you. Attachment to certain people and certain places will eventually affect your health slowly but surely. We must learn to be deliberate with what we eat, what we think, where we go and who we associate with because they all can have either a negative or positive impact on our health. If you know that God cannot be included in what you do, then you have no positive reason to be there. Learn to include God in all things as it relates to maintaining your health!

Heavenly Father, you desire that I remain in prosperity and good health. Lord, I ask for your healing touch even now and deliver me from all maladies, sicknesses, illnesses, pain and spiritual wounds afflicting my body, mind and spirit. Help me to be intentional in maintaining my health. Help me to use wisdom concerning my consumption, the places I go and the people I am in relationship with. Do an overhaul in my life Lord so that I can be healthy and strong to serve you wholeheartedly in Jesus name Amen.

Dealing with a **Heavy Heart**

The world is filled with people who are laden with a heavy heart. There are times when unpleasant experiences leave us with a heavy heart. Too often a person who is oppressed with a heavy heart choose to end their life. Some will seek counselling, while others try to drink, overdose and indulge in risky sexual behaviors to ease their burdens away. A heavy heart is not the easiest thing to live with and people long to be rescued from it. How about you? Do you have a heavy heart? Are you deeply saddened by the tortures of life? Do you find yourself not laughing or smiling? Do you feel suicidal? Chances are you do have a heavy heart.

There are many therapists and professionals available who try to assist people with the problems of a heavy heart. Medications are offered in conjunction with strategies of "talk therapy". These can help to some extent, but medications cannot help spiritual issues. We are spirit beings, housed in a body and issues of the spirit man needs spiritual interventions. A person burdened in the spirit is seeking a permanent solution, not a temporary fix. The question you need to ask yourself is this: Do you desire temporary relief or permanent freedom?

Jesus is the Master Professional that can set the captives free. The Scriptures state that **"whom the Son sets free is free indeed".** Jesus is the Great Physician who has helped many who were demon oppressed and gravely saddened. The Prince of Peace brought peace to the lives of many including mine.

We all need to be transparent about our situation. Nobody knows one hundred percent exactly how another person feels inside except that individual. We may never feel that safety to tell another person the real deal, but we can open up to Jesus and let him know. The Lord will never share our secrets, but He will listen to us and if we ask Him to send the help we need, He will. Jesus is a specialist in heavy hearts. He came into contact with multitudes of people with different issues. I am sure that the heavy hearted gained deliverance and new songs of praises ushered from their hearts. Jesus witnessed the multitude like sheep without a shepherd. He helped and delivered the demon possessed crazed in the mind. I am sure the woman who had an issue of blood for twelve years, cried often to be free from the heaviness of blood flowing from her womb and the heaviness of heart wondering if she would ever be healed. The blind, deaf and dumb must have had days of heaviness in their hearts wishing to be free from their dilemma.

Jesus is willing to help free those who are burdened by a heavy heart because he promises to give those who are laden REST. ***Even now by faith I speak REST to your heart and may PEACE replace heaviness in Jesus name AMEN***. Although we may never meet, with faith in Jesus all things are possible if we only believe. I believe the best antidote for a heavy heart is prayer, singing unto the Lord and the living in WORD OF GOD. In addition, we should stop rehearsing how hurt we feel and ask Jesus to feed our hearts with the peace it needs.

Lord, needless cares we carry, burdening ourselves with a heavy heart when we can take our issues to you and leave them at your feet. Rescue me Good Shepherd from this heavy heart. I need rest from these sorrows. Let your peace fill me up daily in Jesus name Amen.

Power over **Hindrances**

For whom the Son sets free is free indeed! God wants us to be free from all sorts of hindrances. Hindrances are blockages that seek to stop us from getting to the Promise Land of our divine destiny. *The thing about hindrances is this: They can be either internal or external in nature.*

Internal hindrances include doubts, negative self-talk, fears and all sorts of other issues such as our past experiences, which ruminate in a person's mindset. These internal hindrances aim to undermine our efforts and our progression. The more a person agrees with their internal negatives, the more a fortress of hindrance is built around them. External hindrances are those issues and circumstances which involve people or systems that fight against the purpose and destinies of others. These external hindrances come in various forms such as: incorrect relationships, jealousies from others, poverty, power struggles on the job and even people within the church.

The struggles of hindrances are very real, but we have the power of God to push forward and overcome them. When we realize that God is greater than what we face, we side with God because He promised us that ***"no weapon formed against will prosper"***. We can pray to our Father God in the name of Jesus and ask God to deal with all the hindrances we face. Hindrances only seek to kill, steal and destroy our destiny, trying to cap our potential from rising. We must learn to fight them in the power and authority of God! Speak to every internal and external hindrances and tell them to bow, flee and die in Jesus name Amen.

Blessed Father, your Word is right, strong and true. Lord, I ask of you to demolish completely every internal and external hindrances that seek territory in my life. I put them to you Lord for you are willing to clear my path from all obstacles and you will guide me to gain success for your glory. I submit to the power of God and I speak to all known and unknown hindrances to be ye removed in Jesus name for greater is He, Jesus the Lamb of God, living in the inside of me, than anyone or anything in this world that seeks to hinder me or my destiny. This I pray in Jesus name Amen.

The Reality of **Imperfections**

Not too long ago I went shopping for fruits and vegetables and whilse searching through the stacks and stacks of tomatoes I was aiming to find the best looking, most perfect tomatoes. It felt like I was looking for the first finest looking tomato for about twenty minutes. My search was relentless when I heard the Spirit of God said to me: *"You do not live in a perfect world and you will not find a perfect tomato"* That was a wake-up call for me. I don't know about you, but I have the tendency to want perfection, but I have to remind myself that the reality is: **I do not live in a perfect world and so I must expect imperfections from people, things and situations but perfection only from God.**

Only God alone is perfect. We are not perfect. And so, because imperfect people live in this world, we all have some type of flaw and we will inevitably make mistakes. We cannot beat up on ourselves or on others when we or when they err, but we must learn to learn from mistakes and not to repeat them. God has a way of turning our mistakes into ministry and evolving our messes into masterpieces for His glory. Our mistakes are a testimony of our imperfections, but they can also reveal the perfect power of God's hand in our lives. These mistakes can be a lesson or a springboard for others, signaling them to take notes of our mistakes and not to make them their own.

Be thankful to God even for your imperfections shown through mistakes because through them you can gain strength and wisdom to reach higher heights in life.

Heavenly Father, you alone are God the most perfect One, making no mistakes. And so Father, we thank you that you can take our imperfections and errors and use them as teachable moments to us and others. Help us to be stronger and wiser, fortified in our Spirit, as we move from imperfections to becoming your glorious masterpieces on this earth in Jesus name Amen.

God loves **Innocence**

Here is a nugget of wisdom and hope about innocence.
"Innocence and purity of heart is what God loves and absolutely uses for His glory"
~Heather Hope Johnson~
I encourage you to take some time and meditate on the statement above. God is all about purity of heart and innocence. His love breathes innocence and purity. When we look at new born babies and young children who are innocent, we see the purity on display in the way they look, speak and behave. They reflect the Spirit of God upon them. We have the ability to live with a pure heart and this innocence will reflect through us. God wants to use people with a pure heart who worship and live for Him in Spirit and in truth. Ask God to help you to live in purity, not naively, but with innocence and truth.

Heavenly Father, this world is riddled with those who are evil minded and evil in heart. It is your love and purity that makes us innocent. We desire to live a life that is truthful and pure and so we ask you to touch us with your love so that we reflect your innocence like that as a humble child in Jesus name Amen.

Overcoming **Jealousy**

This is a topic that I know well enough and I am certain you have had your bout of being envied or being a tad jealous of another. There are several accounts of jealousy found in the Scriptures. I believe Satan wears the face and heart of jealousy. In the book of Isaiah, we see Satan wanting a position that only belongs to God. Satan wanted the esteemed and glorious position of God's throne. Satan wanted the glory and adoration God was receiving. After all, God is great and His awesome works are to be magnified and praised and the glory that God was getting satan became envious about. This jealousy that satan displayed, moved him to try and overthrow God. But satan's objective was overthrown and he was the one thrown out of heaven. This is what jealousy does. It drives one to want what another has to the extent a person will go to great lengths to gain the position and the possessions of another. This must not be the case for us. We must not be jealous or envious of others.

The bible clearly states that *"envy rots the bones"*. The envier who envies carries an evil within them that can really rot them from the inside out. That evil spirit of jealousy within the envier can become so bitter and caustic it can actually harm the envier physically, emotionally and spiritually. Jealousy is a rotten spirit and if it is not managed and dealt with, then it can develop into a real problem for a person.

Although people who are envious are battling an evil spirit, those who are envied must learn not to let jealousy from others affect them. I couldn't understand why some people would really want, fight for and wish hard for what another person had without even understanding what it took to have it. I have learned that what is given to me from God is mine because God desired that I have it and therefore I am thankful for it. Whether it be much or little, God wants me to enjoy the blessings given. Know for sure that the blessings that you have are yours. The blessings that I have are mine. We should enjoy what we have rather than be bothered by those who want it.

I am reminded of Jesus carrying the cross. That was his portion. Although Jesus taught with authority and in humility, healed, performed miracles, led the multitude, fed the hungry and raised the dead, his greatest test came when He had to carry the cross and be crucified on it. Jesus' ministry was amazing and I am sure there were many who were jealous of him. They didn't understand how a so called "carpenter's son" in their viewpoint, had such power, authority and wisdom. They wanted what he carried.... the anointing. However, I am sure they weren't willing to die on a cross, be beaten, mocked and scourged. They wouldn't be able to manage it, because it cost too much.

The point is this: Jealous people want what you have but are not willing to pay the price to get it, so don't be bothered by that evil jealous spirit and don't desire what others have if you're not willing to carry the cross they have to carry.

Again, do not to be flustered by people who are envious because they wouldn't be willing to do what is needed to get what they would like. Let us learn to carry our own portion and not be jealous of anyone. We must decide to walk our own path of sacrifice and envy not another. And remember, enviers will reap the bitter consequence of "rotten bones"

Heavenly Father, you understand what jealousy does to people. It is written that "envy rots the bones". Lord, because I do not want to be stagnated with jealousy, help me to not focus on others but to be thankful of what you have given me. Lord, you have blessed me with my own portion to manage, therefore I ask you to grant me the wisdom to do so. As Jesus carried the cross, help me to carry mine and not be moved or shaken by those who are envious of me. This I pray in Jesus name Amen.

Kicking *Bad Habits*

Have you ever heard this saying? ***"Bad habits are easy to make but hard to break?"*** Well, there is some truth to this. I have known people who started some bad habits that cost them their health, their relational intimacy with God, their marriage, their peace, their credit history, their job and the list goes on and on. If they had learned to ***"kick the habit"*** then they wouldn't have ended up in bankrupt situations.

I too had some bad habits and let me tell you: They were not easy to break, but with Jesus, all things are possible. Know for sure that there is an awesomeness with including the Lord in our situations. He is the One who gives us the strength in our weak moments because He becomes our strength once we ask Him to help us.

There are many bad habits that are strongholds on our minds, bodies and spirits. It will take the Spirit of the Lord to give us the victory over them. It is the Lord's strength that makes us strong in our very weak moments and we will need to learn to surrender and ask Him to help us.

Picture yourself on a soccer field kicking a ball far away from you. The harder you kick is the further the ball will move away from you. If you kick the ball without power, then that ball will be within reach. I think of the ball as a habit that needs to be away from you, as a matter of fact, it needs to be out of sight! If you allow the Spirit of the Lord to equip you with strength and power to kick the habit away, trust me, you will be able to kick it out of site to Neverland. But if you believe you can "kick the habit" on your own, thinking you can "handle it" then you will only be moving it within arm's reach. One must always remember that bad habits only depreciate and not appreciate. Bad habits destroy, not build. They don't uplift, nor encourage you to grow, but they stifle and stagnate your progress.

Allowing God to empower you to kick bad habits will take certain disciplines such as: fasting, praying, worshiping, praising, being in depth in His Word, fellowshipping with strong believers and more. These spiritual disciplines will equip your Spirit to gain strength to say a bold **"NO"** to bad habits and even cleanse and change your appetites from them. Are you ready to kick bad habits? It's time to get clean and ask God to help you gain the strength to do so, because with God there is nothing impossible if we only believe!

Heavenly Father, there are some bad habits that I need to get rid of today and so Lord I am asking you to help me on this new journey to rid myself of them.

I cannot do it on my own Lord so guide me as I pray, fast, read the Word, worship and praise your name. Shred and remove everything within me that doesn't resemble you and help me to be built up to be more like you. Fill my Spirit Lord. Break every chain of bad habit and bondage Lord and move me each day into your will in Jesus name Amen.

Learning from **Life Lessons**

⚜

Here is a nugget of wisdom and hope about life lessons.

Hard lessons in life are often helpful for our endurance, strength, character and purpose. We need to be strong in the Lord and in the power of the Lord's might in seasons of hard lessons. Those lessons will develop us to be the person we need to be for what we have to face in the future.

Lord, thank you for the hard lessons I had to face and will need to face. I understand that they are being used for my development in character so that I can fulfill my purpose which will bring glory to your name. In Jesus name I pray Amen.

Living *Your Life*

Here is a nugget of wisdom and hope about living your life.

Never allow anyone to hold you hostage from living your life the way God intended. God has an awesome plan for your life but there will always be people who do not understand what God is working out through you. You should not allow others to hinder you from living your life to the fullest. Think about it this way: Why should they have their life and yours also? Let Jesus be Lord of your life in every area of your life. The worst thing you can do is give your power and life over to another person who is incapable of helping you live your best and happiest life. Amen.

Lord God of Heaven, help me to live my best life the way you planned and intended. Help me not to give my life to others but to be guided totally by your Holy Spirit in Jesus name Amen.

Learning How to **Love**

Love. It is what all human beings need. Every person has some sort of desire to be loved. I heard a friend of mine said it clearly several years ago when I visited her. She said: ***"I think I have been created to love"*** When she said it, I was taken aback by her statement but this statement speaks such volumes of truth. We were created to be loved and to love and when we lack love we tend to go looking for it in all the wrong places.

Working with children can be very revelatory. In working with them I notice how most of them need that nurture and attention. They feed off of it and they always come back for more. As adults, we are no different from children. We are children of God. We like love, we thrive from it and we always desire more. You see, the right love (not perverted lust) has a way of making us flourish, develop and blossom spiritually, emotionally and even physically. It takes an open heart to receive love and an even more open heart to give love. When we learn to receive and give love, we gain the opportunity to experience the beautiful benefits of love.

I love to see God ordained covenant couples and God ordained wedded couples in the *"love state of mind and heart"* It reflects on the man and woman in so many ways. They are free with offering affection to each other and you will notice that there is a continuing flow of giving and receiving between the two.

Being in the *"love state of mind and heart"* is a beautiful experience but not everyone gains the chance to experience its depth and power. You see, too many people search for love in all the wrong places rather than allowing the Spirit of God to ordain the relationship. People confuse love with a feeling, when love is more than just a physical reaction towards a person. When we don't allow God to arrange our intimate relationships, we will end up disappointed, frustrated and discouraged. We need not chase after what God can orchestrate. Too many people are in a rush to be loved, when they don't love themselves enough. Loving yourself doesn't mean being selfish. If you are a selfish person and enter into a relationship with another selfish person, that relationship is already at an end before it began. Love and selfishness are on two different wavelengths on different islands and they will never be best friends with each other. Love should always be reciprocated, but too many people are much too selfish to engage in a loving relationship that requires giving of themselves to another.

If your heart, mind and spirit are filled with pure love, then you will eventually attract the power of pure love to you and this may take time.... God's time. How big are you willing to love? It shows up in the quality and quantity of your giving. People tend to love with limits. This means that what is the best for them is not always the best for someone they like or love. They have been hurt in the past and so they put a "cap" on loving BIG! God loves us in big ways and he wants us to do accordingly. Loving big doesn't mean you have to purchase expensive things to prove your love. Loving big means to give your very best. This is what God did. He gave His best by sacrificing His only Son Jesus for us. Would you not say that God showed us how much He loved us? He did, through the sacrifice OF HIS ONLY SON. Are we willing to make the sacrifice and love big by making sacrifices for the ones we love?

The Lord revealed to me that through the Scriptures that the level of our giving is in direct correlation to the level of our loving! We see it with Jesus laying down His life for us so that we can accept this gift of love to be in a relationship and have eternal life with God. We see how Jacob was ready to work extra years to have Rachel as his wife. We notice how Boaz went the extra mile to secure Ruth. We notice how the three Hebrew boys weren't willing to bow before idols to dishonor their love for God and were willing to die by fire. The quality of your loving is a reflection of your heart! When we give of ourselves and of our resources, it reveals the contents within the heart. What type of love is resting in your heart? Is it minimal or abundant? Is it pure love or pure selfishness?

Know for sure that you may try to fool others but you cannot fool God. You may try to fool some people, but you cannot fool everybody. We are revealed by what we do and say and people will see you for who you are. God wants us to wrap ourselves in His love so that we can love others in purity and truth.

Heavenly Father, thank you for your sacrificial love through the offering of your son Jesus Christ. You showed us how to love selflessly and not selfishly. Father, I ask you to help me love freely and to freely receive the love you send my way. Fill me with more of your love in Jesus name Amen.

Manifesting *your Purpose*

You are not a mistake. Your life has meaning and purpose and it must be manifested. Let today be a turning point in your life to manifest the meaning of your being.

Our Creator God took the time to first think of us in His Eternal Mind and then He put his thoughts to action and created us. He breathed life into us and birthed us. When we view ourselves observing the gifts, talents and abilities that we hold, know for sure that they are all the handiwork of the mastermind of God. Whether you or others approve of who you are, let it be known that God created you just the way He wanted. As the Scriptures state: **"We are wonderfully and reverently created."**

God didn't create us to abandon and leave us purposeless. We all have a purpose to fulfill. Some may have a great work to do, where they gain all types of recognition. Others may work behind the scenes not getting any attention or awards, but let it be known that each life on this planet is important and relevant.

Despite many who have faced a rocky childhood, unbearable teen years, or awful experiences riddled with pain and shame during adulthood, let it be known that it is never too late to ask the Lord for help to turn your life around in order to manifest your purpose. Your life was made for a purpose. My life was created for a purpose and we must do everything in our power to manifest our purpose. It begins with asking the Lord to help us, because He is our beginning. One of our main purposes of existence is to have a relationship with the Lord. How can the "created" be successful in manifesting purpose, outside of a meaningful relationship with God who is the "Creator"? Some people will argue this point stating that many have manifested their purpose without God. This is not totally true. Excelling in your purpose doesn't mean you are experiencing the FULLNESS of your life purpose. Certainly, a person can become the top surgeon, judge, professor, nurse, businessman etc., but are they at complete joy, peace, and sweet satisfaction in that success? Success never guarantees peace, joy, love etc. because only God can grant these and no money can purchase them. Amen. There are many people who have success externally, but are defeated internally and spiritually, not enjoying life to its fullest. Money cannot buy love because God is love and only He can give or send love, joy, and peace of mind, health and so much more that can make a person satisfied. Having the aforementioned is a big part of manifesting our purpose and we need the Lord in a big way to help us gain them.

Intimacy with the Lord is needed to manifest our purpose. When we include God in all that we do and build an intimate relationship with him, we in essence become pregnant with his Spirit with the things He wants us to birth on the earth. God has birthed us on earth to birth His will through us on earth. When Mary became pregnant with the Son of God, Jesus Messiah, it was the doing of God. The Lord God overshadowed Mary with His Spirit and impregnated her divinely with His life. Not many believe that a virgin can become pregnant, but what they don't want to embrace is that we are looking at a miraculous great God who can do great miraculous works and miracles were not meant to be understood and explained, but to be believed. This marvelous work of God's hand performing this miraculous conception, brought forth a miraculous Savior who performed miracles. Jesus' birth was a miracle and He came forth performing all types of miracles on the earth. Some believed, others didn't, but that doesn't change the fact that Jesus worked wonders and the Holy Spirit still works wonders through us on this earth. Amen!

In a sense, we too are virgins, impregnated by the Spirit of God to do things we haven't done before. I am an example. I didn't gain any formal education to write books, yet I believe I was born to write and do the work of the Lord. God saved me, filled me with His Spirit, called me to do His work and overshadows me when I write, speak, teach and do His will. We are to manifest the will of God on the earth realm despite what we have faced in our lives. It is written that **"the whole creation yearns for the manifestation of the sons of God".** Let us manifest the reason for our being and bring glory and honor to the Most High God.

Heavenly Father, thank you for creating me, saving me, calling me and impregnating me to do your will on the earth realm. With you as my guide, I will manifest the purpose of my meaning for being. I am not a mistake. My life has purpose and I embrace your movements in my life this day and always in Jesus name Amen.

Managing **Moodiness**

※❖※

I am certain you know someone who is moody or you have come into contact with someone who swings into moods. This topic is not directed to those who are diagnosed with ailments such as depression. Depression is a real disorder that affects many and it is my prayer that relief and ultimate deliverance be theirs in Jesus name.

Moodiness is a problem that can get out of hand if not handled properly. I will never forget when a pastor made a remark. He said: "God is not moody!" It was funny when he said it, but it is such a true statement. Can you imagine if God had moods? We would be in trouble. Thank goodness we can depend on the Lord's consistency and continual love towards us.

We are to be mindful of our moods. Yes, every day will not be sunshine in our lives, but we can make the choice to not be altered by what we feel. Our feelings can indeed fool us and so we must be mindful that we are not being tricked into mood swings. Moodiness stifles our joy from overflowing in our lives. And yes, there are some days you want to be quiet and not be bothered, yet we can choose to be quietly set in joy.

Moodiness shows up in the way we behave, speak, work, and communicate with others. In addition, people prefer not to engage much with moody people. I don't know about you, but I don't want to be referred as Mr. or Ms. Moody.

When we notice that our moods are being affected because of exhaustion, hunger, anger or for any other reason, we have actually chosen to give away our joy and peace of mind to a situation. *What I know for sure is this: There are many enemies of our soul which desire to steal, kill and destroy our joy and peace in the Lord. When we give moods the access to cleave to us, then we have given it the victory and we end up in a defeated mindset.* Below is a poem that the Lord gave me to share with you. Read and meditate on it carefully as the Lord speak to your heart.

<u>*Be a Manager of Moods*</u>

❧❖❧

You are a star
You are a gem
You are valuable and precious to the very end
Don't cast your crown nor wear ugly frowns
Don't let the enemy make you into a clown
Remain in God's grace
Put a smile on your face
And never let moods shift you from your royal place
Change your mindsets and change your moods
God wants to immerse you into
His vast spiritual pools
Be more positive and less stressed
For in doing so, you shall be wonderfully blessed!

Decide today that moodiness is not your friend. Ask the Lord to help you to climb quickly out of the moody frame of mind.

Heavenly Father, I ask of you to help me to release moodiness from my mindset. You were never moody and so Lord I desire to be more like you, drawing from your vast spiritual pools of love, joy and peace in Jesus name Amen.

Recognizing **Needs**

As we go about our busy lives, we often come across various types of people. The one thing I have discerned is this: Whether a person is wealthy or within another financial bracket, each person in this life has at least one need. You need to recognize your needs as well as the needs of others? When we recognize needs of others, we can either choose to be passive or active helpers.

What can we do to help others whether we know them or not? For one, we can pray for them. God knows them better than you do and knows in details what they are dealing with. We can whisper a prayer for them and believe the Lord to work things out for them. The little things that we do to help a person can bring such relief to them unknown to us. We can give up a seat to the elderly or to a pregnant woman. We can help someone who needs help struggling with too many bags. We can even offer to buy dinner for the poor or homeless and we can give a smile and a thank you to someone who has been gracious to us.

Some needs are small, while others are beyond our capacity to help, but we can always pray for a person with or without them knowing. We live in a fast paced, ever changing world and many people are selfishly absorbed in their own lives. When people are focused on their needs, they believe they don't have the time, energy or resources to help others. But this is where people miss the blessing and the solution to their own needs. Helping others with their needs in the capacity you can, is exactly what will open the gates of glory to satisfy a personal need. God will honor those who help others. This is what Jesus did. He helped the sick, the possessed, fed the poor, and so much more. And in the Scriptures we see where Jesus never got sick, was never hungry and he lacked nothing. Jesus showed us how to get our blessings by being a blessing to others. Judas, the disciple who betrayed Jesus worked underhandedly against Jesus. Although he was a part of the twelve, he was doing his own side business because he was selfish. You may or may not know what happened to Judas. Judas' sin came upon him to consume him. His sneaky ways caught up with his conscience and he committed suicide. This is what happens to selfish people. They slowly commit suicide because their wickedness of not choosing to help others brings death and doom to their situation. Let not this be your portion. We all need help so let us help others in the ways that we can.

Let us rise to the challenge of recognizing the needs of others and making an effort through prayer, asking God to help those who need help. Ask the Lord to show you how you can help. God in turn will give strategies or even send the right people who are equipped to help the person. As we help others, God will in turn help us.

Lord of Heaven, too often we are absorbed with our own needs and not in tuned with the needs of others. Help me Lord to shift from being selfish about my needs, to helping others with theirs in the way that I am equipped to help. In doing so Lord, I am confident that you will help me with my needs. Thank you Lord for always being our answer to our needs in Jesus name Amen.

Overcoming **Negative Experiences**

I have had some negatives experiences in my life that were quite unpleasant. How about you? Through it all, I learned much about myself, others and life in general. It is a good thing to gain wisdom from the experiences that we had to face.

How do you handle negative experiences? Do you fume and fuss for days, weeks and months? Do you hold on to the hurt for years or do you let it go and learn from them? I have learned that there are lessons that we can learn from the negatives in life if we choose to ask the Lord to show us what we need to learn.

I have learned that there can be positive outcomes and lasting relationships that can be formed out of negative experience. We just have to gain the proper perspective of the experience and find the honey in the midst of the bee hive even if it means being stung by bees. We don't have to react as if the world has ended because of a negative experience. We can respond to the matter rather than react to it. The Lord has shown me that it is best to learn how to resolve situations by dealing with them appropriately. Our first response to every negative experience is to pray and ask God to reveal to you the reason and the meaning for the negative experience. Sometimes God wants us to see a behavior within. Sometimes God wants to create a relationship with whom you have had the negative encounter. Sometimes the Lord wants to shape and sharpen our skills. There are times the Lord is preparing us for promotion and there are certain behaviors we need to shake off to be strengthened to manage the new position.

Negative experiences can become a haunt to a person if they are not mindful of what they rehearse mentally. If this is a problem you are dealing with now, pray and ask God to help you to forgive the person who hurt you so that you can move forward. God desires to heal all spiritual wounds that you are carrying in your heart, mind, spirit and soul. God will grant you healing if you ask Him to heal you. And once healed, you will become stronger and wiser on how to deal with similar negative experiences. You will be empowered to help those who are wounded.

Heavenly Father, there are times when I face negative experiences that inflict wounds that are difficult to forget. But Lord, we know that you are the bondage breaker and the one who is able to heal all of our spiritual wounds. Lord, this day I ask that you heal all wounds that I have within. Help me not to relive the past, to learn lessons from negative experiences and to have greater wisdom to help others in their times of need. This I pray in Jesus name Amen.

Dealing with the **Opinions** *of Others*

Isn't it amazing how people will have an opinion about you without getting to know who you are first? I remember being in a meeting where I spoke up about a certain topic. Another employee asked me a question in regards to my position on the job. When the person learned that I was at a certain level that didn't fit his thoughts his comment was this: "You spoke so intelligently to be in that position. You articulated yourself so well." I smiled at him and affirmed: "I am intelligent and a position doesn't determine or defines who I am"

People tend to define others based off of what they do and what they have without knowing who they are. I am settled in my spirit that if I do end up with or without a Masters or a Ph.D., I know who I am. I am a child of God first. Titles tend to cause separation rather than unity amongst people. People often tend to hide behind titles, power and position as if their title or position is proof of who they are. Some have degrees and no character and to me that is already a failure. A degree can take you to high positions, but it is your character that will maintain you in that position.

When I was a teenager, my Dad often made a comment which I see proves to be true to this very day. The comment was this: "There are many who are educated who act foolishly!" To add to that: "There are many who are degreeless but are extremely brilliant"

The point I want to make is this: Don't allow anyone to define who you are. Their opinions about you should never matter. In their limited thinking, they view you as a hamster on a wheel or a cockroach within a closed box, but you must view yourself as a lion ruling the jungle. It is not what the opinions of others that matter. It is God's opinion of you and your opinion of yourself that matters the most. Stay away from people who think lower of you and cleave to people who see the best in you. If people refuse to build you up, give yourself permission to walk away from the relationship and don't look back nor give an explanation why you left. We must learn to lose ourselves from the opinions of others and be who God has called us to be.

Lord, it is your opinion and the positive opinions about myself that matter the most. Give me the strength to walk away from every grudge and every unfit opinion others have of me. Help me to cleave to You O Lord, as I become the person you have created me to become. In Jesus name I pray Amen.

Is It An **Opportunity** or a Trap?

Here is a nugget of wisdom and hope about opportunity.

I am sure that you are a person who loves when doors of opportunity open for you? I do, but I have learned to be simultaneously cautious about them. Not every door is a door opened by God. Sometimes an opportunity can be a trap to derailment of your destiny.

When doors of opportunities are opened we are given access to places, people and things so that we can show forth and share the gifts, talents and abilities the Lord has given us. Some opportunities are God-ordained, while others can be a trap, a distraction or even a waste of our precious time, gift and abilities. We must learn to discern which opportunities are God ordained and beneficial. Whenever an opportunity comes your way, your first response should be prayer. We must ask God if the opportunity is of His divine will before we accept it. As the Lord leads, follow, but never move until God says you must move.

In addition, we must also learn that some opportunities are for a time.... this means it is a temporary opportunity. Saying "yes" to an opportunity today doesn't mean "yes" for a lifetime. We must be open to the leading of the Lord so that He can move us and shift us towards other opportunities for us to accomplish His divine will.

Heavenly Father, grant me peace in my heart and confirmation in my Spirit when you have opened a door of opportunity for me. Help me to remain open to your will, so that when it is time to shift to other opportunities I will be available. Thank you Lord for all the opportunities that you will send my way in Jesus name Amen.

Following God's **Ordained Paths**

The Lord has a way and formats on how He does things and this includes how he desires to charter the steps of his people. When we choose the pathways and routes that the Lord sets for us, it may not be easy, but necessary. We should endeavor to remain on the routes God wants us to take for undoubtedly, he will guide us and help us.

When we choose to create our own routes and do things our way, we will eventually encounter frustrations, delays, pitfalls and stagnancy. I have learned that when we don't know what to do, we must ask of God and wait for His leadership. God will not give us all the information in one setting. If God simply states for you to "pack up" then do just that, "pack up". If God speaks to you and say "wait" do just that "wait'. When we learn to obey simple instructions and complete that end of the instruction, then God will let you know what next to do. Again, you will not know it all at once, but be satisfied with what God has shown you and told you to do.

It is always best to agree with what God wills for us. After all, He designed us fully for his purposes. We are not our own and we belong to God. The very day when we said "yes" to Him and prayed and asked Jesus to be our Lord, Master and Savior, our lives changed forever. We were telling God that we wanted Him to direct and ordain our paths. It's really up to us to surrender to Him and keep our part of the arrangement. Saying yes to God is agreeing to the plans and strategies the Lord God has in store. It is giving our lives away to the Lord to have His way, all the way in our lives all the time. Are you really ready to surrender and give it all to God?

The wonderful meaning of God being our all in all is that he promises to lead, protect, be with, fight for, provide for and bless us His way. This is the best way to live, journeying this life with God as our hope, living by faith, in love and with wisdom.

One of my favorite Scriptures is: ***"It is better to trust in the Lord than to put your confidence in man."*** When we trust the Lord God with our whole heart, we will not be disappointed, because what God does he does it very well. ***What God does may not resemble anything close to what you had ever imagined, but for sure it is always GOOD!*** Continue to ask God to ordain your steps. Ask him to help you to gain the courage to follow Him as your Good Shepherd who wants only good for you, who will restore your soul, who will comfort you in the valleys and who will strengthen your faith as He walks with you in hope and wisdom all the way.

Heavenly Father, you are my Shepherd who has created and ordained the paths that I must take. Lead me Lord Jesus into the paths of righteousness. Help me to accomplish your will and purpose on the earth and show me how to trust you every step of the way in Jesus name Amen.

Owning **Ownership**

Ownership. It is a word that is truly misunderstood. The Scriptures state that: *"The earth is the Lords and the fullness thereof. The world and they that dwell therein."* This Scripture ought to be a wake-up call for those who believe that they are owners of what they have. **The truth is this: You own nothing, for when you die, you shall leave everything behind.**

My mother is one of my greatest lesson markers. When she was 81 years old, I gave me a revelation that changed my perspective about living this life. She encouraged me to live life, love it, do what we can to help others and make a difference whether in a large way or by impacting one soul. I watched this vibrant educated woman, who had much sass and spunk in her hey days, change to a steady walking, taking it easy, not worried about anything, trusting God in all things person. She realized that all she worked for was good for that time, but she often questioned what all her youthful chase was about. She often encouraged me to enjoy life and fill myself with memories because she never thought that old age would have caught up with her so fast.

Aging has a way of shifting a person's perspective about ownership. When young, we want everything we can get such as: the education, the perfect job, an exceptional marriage, the car, the house, the children etc. But when all that has been achieved, we then realize that all of that become like a vapor soon to disappear.

What we must not forget is this: God owns all things and we are simply entrusted with what we have been given for a certain amount of time. We are not owners. We are stewards. Our responsibility as stewards is to answer this question honestly: ***Have I done the best with what God has entrusted to me?*** We are being tested everyday with the blessings God has entrusted to us. Have we made a difference? Did we help others?

When we entered this world from our mother's womb, we came naked with a holler out of our mouths. God gifted us the ability to take in our first breath of air. Throughout the trajectory of our lives, we may have gained much, such as money and different assets. But at the end of our lives when God takes His breath from us, on that very day we are stripped of our assets, family, power and all that we once thought we ***"owned"*** The Lord God revealed to me that what we think we "own" is really a "loan". Even if you bequeathed it on to other family members it is still a "loan" and no one can take anything with them when they die.

Heavenly Father, I am the owner of nothing. All that you have gifted to me Lord I am grateful for, but help me Lord to be a good steward of what you have blessed me with. Teach me to make good use of my time and talents on earth, as I empower others and make a difference bringing glory to your name, in Jesus name Amen.

Building **Patience**

If you are a patient person, I give you a high five in the spirit right now. But the real deal is this: Many people are struggling to be patient because we are living in a society that offers up the "instant" at the drop of a hat.

Society is spoiling and spoon feeding people the "instant" from all angles. And people love it! When their needs cannot be catered to instantaneously, fuses break through temper tantrums. Impatient people do things that are horrific because they didn't learn how to wait. Have you ever noticed that people are constantly in a rush? They rush to drive, eat, speak, walk etc. The ease of pacing oneself seems historic. When I catch myself rushing I remind myself that it often isn't worth it. Rushing can have you weary and stumbling through life. I have to also remind myself that God isn't in a rush so why should I? Too often we are in such a rush we miss God's directions. Yes, you can get too busy and too impatient that you miss out on what God seeks to show you. God desires for us to learn the life lessons not to just rush and pass through life. God's ways are not to gratify your selfish needs. With God, there are times He will make us **WAIT** because He wants us to grow in Godliness and patience.

God requires that we develop patience. We need to realize that there are some blessings that we have to wait for. Waiting for God's goodness is good reason enough. We must learn to be patient and respect the waiting processes and timespans. It doesn't matter how much we complain through the wait, or get angry or pace, God will not speed up the process or hasten himself because of our lack of patience.

It takes about 9 months for a baby to grow to maturity before birth. This is the expected amount of time for the fetus to develop in the womb before it enters the world. Should the mother decides she wants the baby out of her womb at three months, the child won't live. If something wrong occurs in the womb during the developmental stages, the womb may abort the fetus and the child will die. Proper development is important within the womb for the child to emerge whole. This is the same for us. When things go wrong in the womb of our waiting and developmental stages of our lives, the outcome can be either death or disability. This too is what happens to people who refuse to develop patience. They end up is situations by which they have to start over or end up disabled.

We must allow God to perfect His work of patience in us. Being impatient can abort valuable blessings. In addition, if we don't fully develop during our waiting period, we will not be ready for the places and platforms God has strategically designed for us. God wants to use us to shine His glory and we should not be in a hurry with our development. Learn to be patient!

When we learn to be patient we also develop humility. We will learn to be quick to listen and slow to speak. We will also learn to move and do what God commands. Patience often allows us to view circumstances through spiritual lenses because we need to draw from God's clarity in certain seasons.

Patience helps us to not jump to conclusions or be hasty when making decisions. I am sure you have had days when you made decisions and you could just whip yourself for being too hasty. We must learn how to wait and watch before being hasty. In being patient, we can extend grace to others and to ourselves for things said and for things done that were inappropriate. And patience gives us a level of mature discernment to see the real nature of a person and of circumstances. Learn to be patient, for it is a blessing to learn how to wait.

Heavenly Father, teach me how to wait and to be patient. I do not want to miss your instructions, neither do I want to miss the blessings or lessons of being patient. Lord, in being patient you are helping me to develop into the person you desire for me to become. Help me to get out of the rushed rat race and to slowly and stealthily depend on your movement as I wait patiently on you. This I pray in Jesus name amen!

Living, Loving and Keeping **Peace**

Here is a nugget of wisdom and hope about peace. Nothing in this world beats the pure and perfect peace of God. Jesus, who is called the Prince of Peace is the giver of peace. We cannot buy peace for it is a gift from God. When God has granted you His peace, ensure that you guard it well and hold on to it carefully for it is a precious spiritual asset. Walk away from peace stealers yet endeavor to be a peace keeper.

Heavenly Father, thank you for the gift of peace. You sent your son Jesus Christ, the Prince of Peace to give peace to the world. In this world there are troubles all around, but in you we have peace. Help me to guard and safe keep the peace you have given me because the world didn't give it and I shall not give it away. Help me to be a peace keeper sharing your love with others in Jesus name Amen.

Prepared through **Perplexity**

Here is a nugget of wisdom and hope about perplexity.

When we are in a perplexing circumstance, it can seem like you are in a storm of chaos. We are often clouded and in the dark when we do not fully understand what is happening. God knows all about darkness. It was He who spoke in Genesis: ***"Let there be light" and light did appear.*** When perplexed, have the faith to speak out as God did for **LIGHT**. Light and understanding is what is needed to uncover the truth of perplexing situations. God will indeed shed forth light upon the situation eventually. Pray and ask God to reveal all that is being covered and hidden from you. God sees and knows all things and has the ability to show you the truth about any situation. God is light and in Him there is no darkness. He has the ability to show us great and mighty things which we do not yet know of.

When the Lord God breaks apart the dark clouds of chaotic and perplexing circumstances, we gain clarity and the proper knowledge needed and leadership from Him to move forward. Call upon the Lord Jesus when you are perplexed. He is the Light of the world and He is willing to save and rescue you out of darkness and perplexing circumstances.

When we are perplexed Heavenly Father, grant us clarity, light, leadership and the solutions that we need in order to move forward. You said that when we call upon you, surely you will answer us. Let there be your continual light leading us, for where you are present, we can see clearly. This we pray in Jesus name Amen.

Strengthened by **Prayer**

❧

Prayer is a powerful weapon against enemy strategies and a powerful tool to access the power of God. It is one of the most powerful weapons in conjunction with the Word of God and faith that a Believer can use to impact their lives and the lives of others. Prayer is accessing the awesome power of God to manifest and work on the earth realm. The Lord does not desire for us to live a life of inefficiency, ineffectiveness, nor insufficiency and so God desires that we bow low and look on High as we stretch forth in the Spirit and ask of Him the One who is Immortal, Invincible, and Impossible to fail. Believe in the power of God. Believe in the power of prayer.

We are living in a time where we have to be living on our knees in the Spirit of prayer. For every waking moment, for every breath we breathe, we need to be in prayer.

Wickedness and all manner of evil are on the rise. People are being seduced left and right because they are not in the secret place of the Most High God. The enemy cometh not but to kill, steal and destroy and if we aren't in the Lord's presence often, we are open prey for the enemy. The Scriptures state that we are to pray continually. It shows that when we keep praying we enter into a covenant covering with God who will shield us and keep us in His care under His wings. Prayer is like a spiritual umbrella that hovers and covers us as we move and live and do our daily business. It is our great secret place in God as we are hidden in the cleft of the Rock (Jesus), hidden and safe from harm and danger. Prayer is resting in the bosom of God! Hallelujah! It is our fountain of sustenance that keeps washing and cleansing us from spiritual garbage like envy, pride, anger etc. When we pray we also receive instructions and revelations from the Lord.

Too often we are defeated because we refuse to keep the lines of communication open with God. God has much to reveal to us and say to us and we have that awesome privilege to SPEAK TO AND HEAR FROM the Lord God of this entire UNIVERSE. What in the world is more awesome than that? This was God's original idea to commune with us daily and have an intimate relationship with Him as we include Him in every area of our lives.

It takes trust and faith to speak to the Creator of the universe. Many people may think that we are crazy when we say that we speak to and hear from God. But they are the crazy ones to live life directionless. Jesus, the Son of God communicated every day with his heavenly Father and so should we.

So let me ask you a question. Who do you talk to when you have a situation or crisis and you need direction and advice that is reliable? You may talk to a best friend, a coworker, a spouse, a pastor, a psychologist, a therapist, a parent etc. and chances are they may be able to help you. God can speak through them, but how do you know for sure? How often do you consider talking with God first? You see, talking to another human being has its benefits but talking to just anybody will help you only to a certain point. When we talk to God about it first, he has the ability to align us with the right people who are equipped with what we need help with. This is why it is best to talk to God first in prayer about what we face, then ask God to send the appropriate help we need.

Jesus prayed, "Let thy will be done, on earth as it is in heaven." This is a master key in understanding how to pray. We are to first hear and know what God's will is in heaven before we pray it on earth. This takes discipline to hear and repeat what the Lord has said as we communicate in prayer. God has a will that he desires to manifest on the earth. God is more concerned about our souls and our spiritual wellbeing than anything else you may think of. Too often people are praying about frivolous matters. God wants our souls to prosper and for us to be in good health. If our souls and the souls of our loved ones aren't saved, renewed and transformed, then it will be challenging for us and them to understand the true purpose of wealth and prosperity. Prayer is what we do as a call onto God to bring change in the lives of those we love. And when we pray, we must learn to patiently wait on God to do His work in His timing. Sometimes you will see a quick and sudden change, but sometimes it takes years to see change manifest. We must hold on to faith and believe that God has heard and the change will eventually manifest.

God is a God of movement when we pray. He has unique strategies and design, but remember that God answers prayers His way on His time.

Never be complacent or lazy in prayer. Boldly, vibrantly yet humbly ask God for help for He is a **GREAT GOD** who can never fail and He knows what is BEST for you! Have that granite and gneiss faith in God, praying and knowing that He has heard your prayers.

Heavenly Father, I ask that you increase my faith and boldness when I come to you humbly in prayer for help. Help me not to be shy nor doubt you when I ask of you. You are incredible in power, awesome in wonder, matchless in the things you do and there is nothing impossible for you to accomplish. Lord you care about my soul and the soul of others, for you desire your people to prosper and to be in good health. Transform my soul Lord and I know that all else will be aligned in my life. Thank you Lord for helping me to practice patience as I wait for you to manifest the answers to my prayers in the timing that you have chosen, in Jesus name I pray Amen.

Telling **Pride** *Goodbye*

A spiritually awful place to be is in the ballroom of pride. Being haughty in heart is never a secret because it reveals itself in grand and stylish ways shouting: "It's all about me!"

Sadly enough, when pride trips up a person and they fall crashing to the floor like shattered glass, they are very embarrassed. The Lord wants to keep us from shame and disgrace. He covers us with His love and often warns us, but when we seek to want our own way, He will draw back so that we can learn on our own.

Do you remember this rhyme?

"Humpty Dumpty sat on a wall. Humpty Dumpty had a great fall. All the king's horses and all the king's men, couldn't put Humpty together again."

Well, this is what happens to prideful people who sit enthroned on their established "high place" to be seen in order to be glorified. They eventually become an utter disastrous scenery.

People who are under the mastery of pride have enthroned themselves as lord and often love to be recognized and praised. When they err, they refuse to accept that they are incorrect and often make a scene to prove their abilities. They are highly judgmental of others and are usually blind about their pride. The worse thing anyone can do is encourage a prideful person in their prideful behaviors. Doing so is simply adding fuel to an already blazing fire.

Pride affects people in many ways and that includes their physical and spiritual health. I know people who have died of cancer and different maladies because all they talked about was themselves and what they accomplished. In addition, they were so proud of being right all the time, often being condescending and hurtful to others. They refused to apologize to people they offended. Pride has a way of rotting away relationships as well. You will notice that prideful people are very egotistical and they are often in the midst of strivings and quarrels.

If you are prideful, be careful. Ask God to show you your heart and if any measure of pride inhabits there, ask Him to help you to overcome it. If pride is not evicted, it will take residence and enlarge itself to the hurt of that person and others. And if you are around people who are prideful, be careful. Behaviors are learnt and if one is not grounded in humility pride can become quite contagious. Dormant pride within can come alive and it only takes the wrong people and situations to activate it. Be prayerful about pride and ask God to chip it away and deliver you from it.

Jesus was not prideful at all. He loved people even those who were prideful, but he knew that they needed deliverance. It takes humility to go to God and ask him to help us overcome pride. Satan is the spirit behind pride, because it was an elixir of pride and jealousy that was found in him that made him think he could overthrow and take God's sovereign place in Heaven. Pride will make a person fall from Godly grace to disgrace and so it is best to ask God to give us a good dose of the Holy Ghost so that we will not be caught up in pride.

Open the eyes of my heart Lord and show me if there is any pride that lives within me. Help me to be proud to be a Believer, but humble in heart as you were. Cast out all and every spirit of pride from my heart and be enthroned O Lord and take your rightful place on the seat of my heart. This I pray in Jesus name Amen.

Never **Quit**

Here is a nugget of wisdom and hope about never quitting.

Do not quit on God. He is the only certain security we have in this entire world. The Lord Jesus Christ came from Heaven to this earth to save us and show us the way to live. He loves us very much and desires that we have the awesome chance of exchanging a life of disaster to a life of abundance, which will eventually be transferred into eternal life. Jesus didn't quit carrying the cross. He didn't quit when He died on it for you and for me. And now that He is the risen Savior, seated at the right Hand of Father God, he still won't quit when it comes to helping us through our journey in this life. Yes, life gets challenging at times, and it has its undulating seasons of lack and pain, but if the Lord Jesus endured, so can you and so can I. When you feel like quitting, close your eyes and pray:

"Save me Lord. Save me. Help me Lord. Help me. Strengthen me Lord. Strengthen me."

Heavenly Father, when I feel like quitting, when I feel like I can't go further, help me to close my eyes and ask you for your saving, helping and strengthening power in Jesus name Amen.

Give **Regrets** *an Expiration Date*

In the summer of 2015, I had an interesting encounter and conversation with a 70 year old man named James. Our meeting would have seemed odd, but I knew it was God-assigned. He was on his way to a doctor's appointment that midday and I was on my way to do some banking. But God had designed this meeting for us to meet and talk that day at the bus stop.

I will never forget how he pointed out that I was wearing a ring that was the same design of an earring in his left ear. I actually had noticed that earlier in our encounter as we chit chatted, but he was the one who mentioned it. We communicated about several matters until it became deeper and more personal on his end. God is the Lord of sending us in the deep waters of the hearts of people. As Believers, we are "fishers of men"

James shared that he was married twice and was currently involved in a relationship where the woman didn't want to marry him. But the crux of our meeting unfolded when he disclosed that he had regrets about certain happenings in his life which occurred about forty years ago. I discerned in his eyes the sadness and heart-brokenness he was still feeling due to improper decisions he made earlier in his life. Our encounter ended in prayer, a word of encouragement and he was grateful because he said he felt he had hope to move on especially with renewing his relationship with God.

I can totally identify with what James was enduring because I too had experienced regret and guilt because of many faulty decisions I had made earlier in life which included marriage. Some of these decisions toppled me to the floor, yet I rose above them stronger, all because of the grace, love, mercy and divine help of my loving Lord and Savior Jesus Christ. The Lord had to show me that regret, guilt and shame wasn't going to help me and I had to rise up out of those ashes and become more that the issues and circumstances I faced. Regret, guilt and shame was only hurting me, not helping me.

You see, we cannot change what happened in the past. None of us have a time machine where we can step back in the past and fix what happened then. The past is forever gone, but often relived and rehearsed in the minds of many. Wishing and wondering "if you could do this and if you could do that" is simply a wish and certainly those wishes won't come true. Thinking about the past and wishing to change the past is like chewing on air like how a cow chews its cud. We are to simply leave the past alone right over there in yesteryear and learn to move forward and live now in God. It is best to see what you can do now to make your life matter and bring more meaning to your life and the lives of others.

If you feel as if you can't break the thoughts or the wounds of yesteryears, ask God for help. Ask the Lord to pull up the weeds and plant new seeds in your spirit. Ask God to renew your mind and give you new thoughts. Cry out to God and yield your heart to Him and give him the right to heal you from the inside out. Living in the household of regret is living in bondage. Don't allow satan to torture you any longer for it is written: ***Who the son (Jesus Christ) sets free is free indeed. I decree over you and I decree over myself: BE SET FREE AND BE HEALED in JESUS NAME AMEN!***

Heavenly Father, I need your powerful healing touch that will change my life from hurt to wholeness. Remove all the fractured places of regret in my life and help me to move out of bondage and move forward into my future. I cannot change the past but I can change my mind to do things your way now and so Lord I am expecting a restoration in my mind, heart, body and soul for you are my Redeemer and Restorer. Thank you for answering my prayers in Jesus name Amen.

Being Mindful of **Relationships**

There are all sorts of relationships that tend to come our way. Some are beneficial while others are fruitless. We must be very careful of who we get into relationships with because they can cause us grief in the end. Futile relationships are to be discouraged and we must be discerning enough to identify them when they are presented. There is no need to be bound to insignificant relationships that you know won't benefit you, but will simply waste your time and resources. Learn to be a master discerner of the spirit of people. You know deep down inside your heart and by the leadership of the Holy Spirit when a relationship is going nowhere. Don't wait 5 years to see a relationship end, when you already knew the relationship was a dead end one since the third month of its inception.

When faced with a new relationship, ask God if the relationship was designed by Him. Ask the Lord if and how the relationship will bring meaning and honor to his name before building any type of bond with the person. In doing so, you give the Lord territory to work within the relationship to either bring it to a close or to strengthen it the way he desires. In doing so, you save yourself time, trouble and heartache. I always tell my son that our hearts are precious treasure and we ought not allow anyone to toy with our hearts.

As for relationships that are hurting more than helping, ask God to change the hearts of those within the relationship so that no one will be severely hurt should the relationship needs to dissolve. God wants us to live in peace and so relationships that need to end, I encourage you to ask the Lord for divine assistance so that it can end in peace.

Know for sure this one thing about relationships: God is One who is BIG on relationships. He created us to have a relationship primarily with Him. Depending how great and loving our relationship is with the Lord, then our relationship with others will reflect our oneness with God. We can't force people to reciprocate love, but we can be loving to them regardless. And also, we must allow God to ordain and charter the correct relationships our way by His strategic and divine Hand. In doing so, glory will be given to His name. When relationships are covenanted by God, we will experience His presence, His purpose, His productivity, His power and His holy pleasure within it. As Jesus related with people in a loving and sanctified way, let us desire to build relationships as such.

Heavenly Father, you are the author of relationships. We notice how you created us so that you could relate to us and have communion with us. You sent Jesus to be the present God with us and Jesus sent the Holy Spirit to be in us and with us.

Lord, we give you permission to end and remove all ungodly relationships and to build Godly ones so that glory will be given to you in Jesus name Amen.

Reverencing God

Here is a nugget of wisdom and hope for you about reverencing God.

To fear God means to reverence, honor, respect and hold the Lord in high regard. Wouldn't you say that our heavenly Father God, the Lord Jesus Christ and the Holy Spirit are worthy to be respected and honored? Indeed yes.

We are living in a time when people both in the church and in the world do not respect God. They believe and think that it is okay to disrespect God, His methods, His standards and His Words. They think that they can changed what He has written because they no longer think it is relevant or side with their beliefs. God is true to His word and He loves us and has given us the direction that we must take to live life but many seek to disrespect the Lord.

Objecting to God and being irreverent to Him doesn't make man greater than God. It only makes him a fool. Who is greater than God? Show me? There is no one greater than God and eventually those who think their way is the right way rather than God's righteousness, they will face a judgement that they have set for themselves. God cannot be killed even if some people choose to be irreverent to Him. There will be those who will remain faithful to God and will regard God as holy and will reverence Him. Will you be counted in the number? Will you be within that remnant who will choose God and reverence Him? Our reward is sure.

Heavenly Father, help me to continue to live a life of holiness and purity in complete reverence to you and the things of God. Help me to dwell in your presence of love, peace and joy knowing that it is worth it all to revere you. Thank you in advance Lord for the sure reward for those who choose to honor you. This I pray in Jesus name Amen.

Living a **Sacrificial** *Life*

Here is a nugget of hope and wisdom for you about living a sacrificial life to God.

There comes a time in our lives when we have to make sacrifices. We cannot run away from or avoid making sacrifices. Whether it be making a sacrifice to reduce debt, improve health, going back to get a higher education or doing what needs to be done for family, the life of sacrifice is real. It takes discipline to make sacrifices in order to see positive changes. *Sacrifices may not come easy, but often sacrifices are necessary.*

Jesus sacrificed his life for us. He laid down his life, gave it up, so that we can live. What do you have to sacrifice today? What do you have to give up in order to see a positive change for good? I had to sacrifice relationships and pleasure to live the life God wanted for me. When we want the best, we have to sacrifice good and better to gain the best. We need to learn how to sacrifice and do what needs to be done in a Godly Spirit led way to gain what the Lord has prepared for us.

One thing I have learned in this journey being a Believer is this: ***"It often takes a life of sacrifice to be settled in Christ."*** <u>We have to remember that when we said "yes" to God, that "yes" was a direct "no" to other things, people and lifestyles.</u> Saying "yes" to God often means slaying our flesh and our needs and saying "no" to our will. "Yes" to God is stating: ***"Let thy will be done Lord in my life. Amen"*** *We surrender what we want for what God wants.* Look at what Jesus prayed in the garden before his ordeal of the crucifixion: ***"Not my will, but thy will be done"*** Jesus was saying "yes" to God to endure the cross, despite how hard and treacherous it was to become for him in a few hours. Are you saying "yes" to God? It means sacrifice!

Heavenly Father, your son and our Savior Jesus Christ said "yes" to You. He sacrificed his life so that we can have life. Lord, when you want us to grow and develop into the person you intended, help us not to be afraid to say yes. Grant us the strength to say "yes" unafraid and to carry our own crosses despite the gruesomeness in Jesus name Amen.

Dealing with Different **Seasons** of Life

Here is a nugget of hope and wisdom about dealing with the different seasons of life.

Life has seasons. Yes it does. Our lives constantly change and we must be versatile in the Spirit to deal with the different changes that come our way. I am certain that you have often come across someone who is "stuck in their past". Yes, they talk about the hurt, the pain, the shame, the heart break and they have difficulty to move forward.

God designed us to move forward. We age up, grow up, and must mature up! Different seasons of life, whether challenging or positive, must be dealt with and they give us the opportunity to develop. It is up to us to learn the different lessons that we are being taught. These lessons are giving us the opportunity to MATURE SPIRITUALLY!

When we face seasons that seem relentless, we must keep our focus on the TRUE AND LIVING GOD! We must stand firm in faith, giving God all the praises even through the stormy seasons. We must remain steadfast in prayer and allow the Word of God to rule our emotions. When we come to the realization that

God is greater than anything and everything we face, we will be unshakeable, unmovable and unstoppable through scorching summer seasons, blistering winter seasons, pollen ridden spring seasons and shedding autumn seasons. Place our Lord and God as King over all the seasons we face Amen.

Heavenly Father, we place you at the highest place as Lord over all the affairs and seasons of our lives. We know that you are stronger and there is no power that supersedes yours. Let us keep strong in the Lord and in the power of Your might. Let us have our determination set as flint, solid in you. We trust you with all of the different seasons of life in Jesus name Amen!

Seeking God

Here is a nugget of hope and wisdom about seeking God.

We are to be a people who seek the Lord with our whole hearts and put Him first above all things. Not many will agree with this, because too many opt to put a career, a vision, an education or even those whom they love before the Lord. But this is a grave mistake that can be very disappointing to those who practice this.

You see, we must always begin with God for He is our very beginning. It is not a job that is our beginning, nor a spouse, nor a child or an education. These things and people have their positions, but God is the one who has blessed us with these added benefits. Our life began with God and therefore He desires that we put Him at the helm of the life He gifted to us. He gifted us LIFE and therefore we are to SEEK God for all things.

It is written in the Scriptures, that we are to ***"Seek ye first the kingdom of heaven and His righteousness and all things will be added unto us."*** Let this marinate in your heart.

"Seek ye FIRST the kingdom of heaven and His righteousness..."

We were first in the mind of God before we became a reality on this earth. He designed plans that carries added blessings. God wants us to have His best manifest in our lives. Too often we miss out on them because we get consumed with:

"Chasing after what we want RATHER than seeking God's will"

God is the all sufficient One and He will grant us what we need. The beggar, blind Bartimaeus knew the power of seeking God. He chased Jesus with his voice, crying out to Him for mercy. And he certainly gained the attention of Jesus who asked him what he wanted. Bartimaeus responded "to regain my sight", which was an appropriate request because Jesus came to heal, deliver and restore. Jesus honored the beggar's request. Bartimaeus received his sight because he sought God's will. Are you seeking God's will or are you chasing what you want? It's time to seek and ask the Lord to give us His "sight" for in doing so we will accomplish His will. We need to rise up out of spiritual blindness and gain Godly righteous vision.

Heavenly Father, too often I have chased after what I wanted rather than seek after what you have willed for me. Help me to gain the right vision to see what you desire for my life and help me to come into alignment with it. Lord Jesus, help me to put you first in all things for you are my very beginning and so I must always begin with you. This I pray in Jesus name Amen.

Say So long to **Selfishness**

⚜

Here is a nugget of hope and wisdom for you about selfishness.

The world is a breeding ground filled with selfish people, but you don't have to join that crowd. What I know for sure is this: ***"Selfishness is a picture of immature love."*** People who are self-absorbed are bankrupt to giving love. You see, love knows how to ***"let go"*** and be about a life of ***"living for giving"***, but selfishness stretches out its hand like a pauper and says: ***"give me, give me, and give me more"*** even if the person already has manifold blessings.

Selfishness is a spiritual disease that needs a remedy. The remedy for selfishness is to have a spiritual heart transplant of love. Only the Spirit of the Lord can do this, for God is love.

It takes sacrifice to get out of the mindset and heart-set of selfishness. It takes a divine movement of the Holy Spirit to reveal to those who are selfish that a change is needed.

Jesus was not selfish at all. He was always concerned about people and made it happen for those who were in need. If they were hungry, he found a way to feed them. He met with a woman at a well who was thirsty in Spirit, and after conversing with her and offering her "living water", she accepted and He filled her up. Another case where Jesus proved that love is the remedy of selfishness was when He met up with a woman who was caught in the act of adultery. He could have said: "She's guilty! Stone her" but he saved her. Jesus was about the welfare of others and selfishness was not his ministry. He ministered selflessness. When we choose to lay down our lives for others as led by the Spirit of the Lord, this is the ultimate act of selfless love.

Are you selfish? Really take some time to reflect on yourself. Are you always thinking that it should always be "all about you?" If "yes" then my dear you are selfish. God wants to transform selfish people and empower them to help others. But if you have this *"me, me, me"* attitude then you need to spend some time in prayer, because it really isn't about you! It's about what God wants to do through you for others.

Selfish people are in a "nest" with their "fishy self" and people will end up leaving them slowly but surely. If this is your time to give up selfishness, pray this prayer below.

Heavenly Father, if you have identified that I am selfish, I need for you to transform my life and my spirit today. You laid down your life selflessly so that I can have life and therefore I desire to live the way you lived. Teach me how to give with love and wisdom. Guard my heart from people who desire to deceive and use my love for their selfish purposes. Let me be an example for those whom I come into contact with, so that they see your love through my life in Jesus name Amen.

The Lust of **Sex**

This message is strategically designed for all those who are in a sexually intimate relationship that God didn't design. God designed sexual intimacy to be within the context of marriage. This is the rightful place where God permits a man and a woman to engage in sexual intercourse.

Too often, humankind wants to do what they consider is "right" or what they "feel to be right". We must understand that just because something seems right doesn't mean it is righteous in God's eyesight. If you are a Believer, and you desire to please God, then you ought to make it your preference to obey God. What God says in His word is not a debate, but a rule of conduct that needs adherence. If you choose to do your own thing, simply ready yourself for the consequence that will come, if you do not turn aside from your ways.

The sex act is an extremely intimate happening. When engaged in this act, you are doing more than merging body parts together. You are merging with the spirit, fluids, past and present with another individual. Sex builds bonds that we often don't see, nor fully comprehend, but they are present and experienced together. Women in particular, find it difficult to move forward from intimate relationships because of spiritual bonds that are not quite easy to break. But with God all things are possible.

What I know for sure is this: Wait patiently for the mate God has called specifically for you. Do not engage in multiple relationships chasing after what God can present to you at the right time. Do not indulge in casual sexual flings, nor indulge in sexual behaviors to attract a partner. You are simply cheapening your value. God has a way of revealing to your mate your value who will honor your value. I have experienced the deceptive luring of the enemy and too often many have undergone awful circumstances because of wanting to be in a relationship. It is good to wait! Wait on the Lord for what He does, He does it and builds it well.

Do you know someone who has fallen prey to the luring and deception of the enemy? They thought a relationship would be all that they wanted, only to either end up broken hearted, abused, ridiculed, exposed, pregnant, sick or worse dead. God isn't apart of these disastrous outcomes. God desires that relationships are blessed and give Him glory.

Jesus had an interesting conversation with a woman at a well. She was there to draw water from the well, but He was there to offer her living water that would spring up in her and fill her need. You see, she was in a relationship with a man, living with him. Jesus even tapped into her personal life and told her that she had

had 5 husbands and the one she was living with wasn't hers. Hmmm? This woman was thirsty for something these men couldn't give her, and so Jesus had to offer her a different type of water because her "thirst" was spiritual in nature not physical in nature. She needed to draw from a different type of well. Not Jacob's well that had H2O, but Jesus' well of living water. Too many women have a spiritual thirst that they think a man can fill sexually. No man can fill what only God can fill. If Jesus hadn't step into her situation, she probably would have ended up in a tragic place. Thank God he did!

Listen to me, single, divorced and widowed women: Receive this warning. Do not surrender to the lusts of the flesh and yield your body upon the altar of a bed to a man who isn't your husband. He is only feeding on your body and possibly dumping garbage in your spirit. Too often women are so desperate to have a companion, that they disregard their values and open up themselves as a supermarket, allowing a man to go shopping, taking what he wants for free without any real commitment. Don't allow leeches, in the form of a human being to suck the life from your body and spirit. You are not a socket for him to push his plug in to gain energy from you. Learn to employ self-control and ask God to help you maintain a life of purity, set apart for God's use. Ask God to control certain sexual excitements and appetites. God will help you and perform the necessary adjustments in your body, only if you ask Him. Learn how to wait on

God for the partner God has planned and created just for you. When God determines that you both are ready to receive each other, the presentation will occur at the proper time. You will both know that you belong to and meant for each other. Amen.

Heavenly Father, help me to patiently wait for the covenant partner that you have designed and destined just for me. Help me to operate in self-control as I master the flesh by allowing the Holy Spirit to lead me into the correct relationship. I will not surrender my body upon any altar to be used for unrighteous sexual acts, but to stand in righteousness until the day you have allowed me to enter into the marriage covenant that you have ordained for me. This I pray in Jesus name Amen.

You Lose when **Stubborn**

Here is a nugget of hope and wisdom for you about stubbornness.

Picture yourself standing in front of a high brick wall. You need to get to the other side but you have no way to go around it, under it, or through it. How do you feel? Yes, STUCK!!

There are such brick walls in our lives and they show up as: our attitudes, mindsets, thought life, and heart set. Sometimes we are standing in front of brick walls and they are making us STUCK.

There is a brick wall that is very dangerous and we must be very mindful of it. It is the brick wall of *stubbornness* and it is a wall that refuses to come down if we don't do everything in our power to demolish it. Stubbornness is a big hindrance that blocks us from the blessings that God has for us. If you desire to gain the blessings of God, I encourage you to remember this phrase about stubbornness: *Stubbornness blocks blessings*.

There are times when God wants to help us and He sends great help our way, but we are too busy being stubborn looking for the blessings to come another route. We are to be flexible in the Spirit, being alert to the movements of God. I sat with an awesome man of God and professor who encouraged me to: Develop an ear for God's voice and heed the voice of the Lord. His words changed my life.

God loves to direct our paths and leads us into righteousness, but if we are stubborn, we risk missing his leadership and help. Check in with your heart and ask the Holy Spirit if any measure of stubbornness lives there. If you determine it does, then ask God through His power to evict it and to replace stubbornness with the willingness to obey His divine leadership. A heart that is willing to receive of Him is a life that is ready to be blessed by Him!

Heavenly Father, stubbornness is an evil spirit of my will to steal and block your blessings from my life. I give you full control Lord to evict it out of my life, mind, spirit and will so that I willingly submit to your leadership. In doing so, I will be ready and open to receive from you. This I pray in Jesus name Amen.

Don't Sit on Your **Testimony**

Sometimes, we get ourselves in matters that are not of the Father's business, but even so, the Lord has a way of turning our past painful experiences into a testimony. Self-induced situations are often linked to the lusts of the eyes, lusts of the flesh and the pride of life. These experiences at times entangle us and give us a good whipping, but thanks be to God that His mercy endures forever.

When God grants us His mercy and deliverance from situations, we often come out learning more about God, ourselves, others and life. God gives us powerful testimonies so that we can share and help others. Do you have a testimony? I have many and we are to share what God has done for us and through us so that we can offer others hope to overcome. Our testimonies give others living hope proving that God is powerful enough to work on their behalf.

What I know for sure is this: ***God can do anything once it doesn't violate His laws and principles***. Testimonies encapsulate the ingredients that prove the power of God. God is not a weakling and it is His power that triumphs the wickedness of satan. ***Do not be afraid or ashamed to share your testimony.*** Who cares what others think of us for what we have done or didn't do? What is greater is that God has done a remarkable work in our lives and He has helped us to overcome. That is what matters the most. Our testimonies are our truths of God's redemptive and restorative power and they are a stark reminder that we overcome by the blood of the Lamb and by the word of our testimony! Amen!

Heavenly Father, your power never changes and you are the same yesterday, today and forever. Thank you for working out situations on my life and for granting me a testimony that I can share with others. Help me to declare your name, your love and your goodness. Help me to talk about your awesome wonderful movements in my life. Surely Lord you are powerful and there is none life you in Jesus name Amen.

Waiting on God's **Timing**

Here is a nugget of hope and wisdom about God's timing.

God is on the clock, but not limited to time. Do you agree with this? There are millions and possibly billions of people in this world who are in a rush to accomplish goals. They are in a race with time to get a career, a business or a ministry off the ground. They want to get married and start a family or want to retire and travel the world. Some people have a set timelines and deadlines for their lives, to the extent they refuse to incorporate God in any of these goals. When these goals aren't met, disappointments and even depression sets in like a pearl in any oyster.

God is never late if we learn to submit our plans to Him and be willing to reshuffle what we want to what God requires of us. We have to learn to be led by God's Spirit. His ways are not our ways. His plans for us are at times different to what we desire.

God knows exactly how to work things out. Yes He does. He has the ability to do so, because He knows and sees the complete details of everything that concerns our lives. ***If you think that God*** *doesn't know your tomorrows or your ten years from now, this is your <u>wakeup call</u>ß "<u>Cock-a-doodle-doo!!!</u>"*

God created us and He wants us to walk into the plans He has designed exclusively for us and not be entrapped by the devils deceptive diversions.

Never rush ahead of God and shake yourself off from lagging behind His movements. He wants us to be in alignment with Him and what His plans are for us. He is our Shepherd and we must allow ourselves to be led, not to try and lead God into agreeing what we want for our lives. That is simply ridiculous to try to think above what God knows is best for us.

God is the Master of time. He instituted time and He knows how to manage it. We often like to set goals with the intentions to accomplish our well-manicured "to do" lists. Well, God has a way of shifting all that around, much to our disappointment. Because we don't know what tomorrow holds, we are to rest confidently that God who holds tomorrows in His Hands, knows what is best and therefore we should consult Him about all things. Ask God to help you as it relates to what you should be doing at this particular time of your life. He will reveal it to you and help you to get on track and to be on time.

Heavenly Father, there are times I desire to do things my way in my timing. Your times and my times are not the same and so I desire to be in alignment to do what you have planned for me and in the time

I need to accomplish it. Help me not to rush ahead of you, nor lag behind, but to keep in stride with you. Grant me enough time to do what needs to be done so that glory and honor will be given to your name in Jesus name Amen.

Trusting God *with Your Whole Heart*

God wants us to place our full hope and trust in Him. We were not designed to live life alone or by chance. We were designed to rest securely and confidently on God. In the book of Genesis, God walked with Adam in the cool of the day in the garden. In the Gospels of Matthew, Mark, Luke and John, Jesus promised the Holy Spirit to be in us and to walk alongside us. From the beginning of time, God always desired to have an intimate, loving and trusting relationship with His best creation, Mankind.

We tend to trust in things and people a little too much. These do not offer a permanent guarantee, because situations and people often change. And when they do, especially for the worse, we can become very disappointed and distraught. The Scriptures guide us in Proverbs that we must:

"Trust in the Lord with all of our hearts** and **lean not on our own understanding. In all of our ways to acknowledge Him and He will direct our paths straight."

In Psalms 118, we become aware of who to trust:

***"It is better to trust in the Lord** than to put confidence in man."*

It is evident through these Scriptures that it is always best to trust the True and Living God with all of our hearts. In doing so, we shall be in the ***"safe zone"***

I was amazed to witness trust and faith in action through a 3 year old little girl. The children were at play in the play yard and this little girl decided to climb up some wide metal simulated stair cases, which demanded the use of her hands and feet. As she ascended the stairs carefully, she came to the turning point and I saw that she encountered some difficulty to move forward. She decided to call for help. I went to her rescue, not in an attempt to save her, but to give her strategies on how not to give up but to finish her goal of reaching to the top. I wanted this event to be a lasting teachable moment for both her and me. As I guided her hands and feet, she attained her goal slowly, safely and securely. She was quite ecstatic about this and decided to redo the task. As she ascended again, she did so carefully as I stood in close proximity by her side, guarding her but not holding her. She came to that same turning point, but this time she decided to stand up boldly. As she did, she balanced herself, laughed fiercely as if to say: "I have conquered you turning point!!!!" The once difficult turning point for this child became a place of fierce laughter. It was the funniest sight, and I too laughed fiercely alongside her, because I knew the only reason she was so bold to stand at such a dangerous turning point for her little size, was because I was present ready to assist her. She trusted my ability to help her. She trusted my heart that I wouldn't allow her to fall. She trusted me. After her victory laugh and victory stance, she went up the ascent again and again, like a hiker at ease conquering Mount Everest!

That experience taught me a lot about trusting God. There are times in our lives when we have to face a turning point and it can be quite a difficult ascent that seeks to grip us with fear. God wants us to trust Him and his heart towards us that He will not allow us to fall because he wants us to trust His proximity. Too often we don't move forward because of fear, but God wants us to trust Him.

Here is a word for you: Do not be afraid to trust God. Place all that you fear in His care and in His hands. Put yourself in God's care for he cares for us and doesn't want us to fall. We can put our guarantee in His heart towards us that He is there, close-by to guide us and to guard us up and along the ascent.

The Lord revealed to me that we trust Him in ways that we often do not think about. Our heartbeat, breathing, circulatory system, ANS and PNS are all in His charge. We don't ask God every day to let our heart beat or to help us to breathe. We trust Him automatically in these areas. It just happens normally. Now we are to take that same trust and put the rest of our lives in His care, knowing that when we trust Him, He will make the best happens for us.

Heavenly Father, help us to trust you automatically. Help us to trust your heart towards us, because it is good and you desire that we conquer challenges and achieve the goals you set for us. Help us to sense your presence, knowing that you care for us in the minute areas, as well as, the turning points of our lives. Help us to completely surrender to you, to stand up in faith victoriously and laugh in the face of challenges because there is no challenge that is bigger than your power. Lord have your way in our lives, for in doing so, you will work out what is best for us always. This we pray in Jesus name Amen.

Being **Used** *by God*

❧❖❧

God is a God of purpose and He has a way of assigning special purposes for certain people. We all have a purpose that we need to accomplish before we leave this life. Some discover it. Others evade it while some accomplish theirs. Everything God does, he does it for a purpose and God doesn't desire for us to live a purposeless life. Your life has purpose.

Many people try to disregard your life because you may or may not have an academic degree. You may even doubt yourself about accomplishing certain goals because you feel like you don't have the necessary qualifications. You may think that you are stuck in your job until retirement, or you will never make it out of poverty. *All these are not truths unless you choose to agree with those lies. Your life has worth and purpose and God desires to use you.*

I am reminded of Jonah. God created him for a special purpose and called him for a special job at a certain time of his life. Jonah chose to run from God's assignment rather than run to accomplish it. *What Jonah didn't consider was: He couldn't*

run and hide from God who created him, his purpose and the world. Where could Jonah hide in this world created by God? The world was God's and so Jonah was in for a lesson he wouldn't forget. God created a great fish that swallowed him up and gave Jonah some down time to think and meditate. Jonah couldn't run anymore but had to agree with the God who wanted to use him. Jonah decided to do what God wanted him to do and when God saw that Jonah's heart was ready, he released Jonah from his fishy situation.

God wants to use you too. When I realized that God created me for His use, the task seemed tremendous, but God showed me that it was to be done in steps and stages. I encountered many hardships, had to redo many tests, learned many lessons, endured lots of heartbreak, witnessed many miracles and saw God transform my life and others in many ways. At the publication of this book, I am persevering to complete my degree and move forward to allow God to use me in the ways He desires. It is never a cruise being used by God, but it is fulfilling to win and to witness others win.

What I know for sure is this: Don't run away from your purpose like Jonah, nor make up excuses of what you don't have to accomplish your purpose. God will make a way, just as how He made a way and parted the Red Sea for the children of Israel to cross over and be spared from Pharaoh and his army.

Once you have the Lord on your side, you have all that you need. The Lord is our all in all. Surrender to be used by God. It is well worth it.

Heavenly Father, too often we calculate what we lack, before we come into agreement with being used by you. Lord, help us to rest in the knowledge that once we have you, we have it all, for you are our all in all. Keep us focused on you and help us every step of the way. Lead us Lord. Transform us Lord. Teach us Lord and tame us, so that we accomplish what you have purposed on the earth realm in Jesus name Amen.

*Filling the **Vacuums** in your Life*

Here is a nugget of hope and wisdom about filling the vacuums in your life.

When Jesus walked the earth, there were many people who were experiencing vacuums or empty places in their lives. One of the biggest and most painful vacuums a human being can experience is the lack of love. God designed us to love and to be loved. When people want to be loved and they want it badly, they often don't seek that love from God first. What happens is they go looking for love in all the wrong places. They try to fill the lack of love in their lives (the vacuum) with all the wrong things.

Some people tend to ingest all types of things to feel good and feel filled. Whether it be using alcohol, drugs, indulging in pornography, abusing sex, money, food, clothes, power, position, entertainment, career, education etc. nothing will satisfy that internal insatiable appetite for more. The vacuums within a person and need for love are not filled by the materials of this world. Vacuums that God created can only be filled by the loving Spirit of God.

Do you have a vacuum and are you trying to fill it with all sorts of things that the world offers? I will be the bearer of good news for you now. What you are seeking is not in the world and you will never find it there. What you are seeking is in God and it is God's Spirit that you need to turn to for a true filling.

The woman Jesus met at the well, had a vacuum in her heart. She was at Jacob's well drawing physical water, but Jesus saw the vacuum in her Spirit that needed living water. Jesus had what she needed. She just needed to ask for it. He offered and she accepted. She became filled with living water! Hallelujah!

Are you in need of a filling of something else than what you have tried? Do you have a vacuum in your spirit and heart? Are you being beaten down by the demands of this life and you don't think there is a solution? Today is your day to drink of the living water that will fill you up. Do you want it? Do you really want it? Then by faith right your answer to this question or say it out loud:

I have a vacuum in my life, my heart and my Spirit and I say (yes or no_____) to the living water that Jesus is offering me right now. If you have said yes to God, by faith say this prayer in the name of Jesus:

Pray this prayer with me.

Heavenly Father, I admit that I have a vacuum in my heart, spirit and life. I have tried what the world offered and it didn't *work. You said that you came to this world so that I can have life more abundantly. I need that life and I need the living water you offered the woman at the well. Lord Jesus, come into my heart, spirit and soul. Forgive me for all the wrongs I have done. I say yes to you today. Live in me and be my Lord and Savior in Jesus name Amen. Sign your name:_____*

Remaining in the **Will of God**

❦

Here is a nugget of hope and wisdom for you about remaining in the will of God.

Meditate on this quote.

"Always seek the perfect will of God and not the permissive will of God. His perfection supersedes His permission."

Really get this in your spirit and understand what it really means.

The will of God is closely tied to your purpose and your destiny. God didn't create you randomly and without purpose. Everything that God has created has a purpose, meaning and destiny. You and I have a reason for being than just existing. We exist for a reason, just as how God exists for a reason.

Many people never realize their meaning for being. They never understood their purpose and so life passed them by like a train. God doesn't desire for us to live meaningless lives, but purposeful ones. Our lives have several connecting points between birth and death. When we discover our purpose during our life journey, the connections make more sense when we remain in the will of God. As Believers, we know that our Good

Shepherd is Jesus Christ. We, who are His sheep, are to surrender to the leadership of the Shepherd. Jesus walked this earth and He became very familiar with the different life terrains that we will face. Christ, in the form of the Holy Spirit is now with us to help us along the way. The person of the Holy Spirit knows exactly how to guide us, but too often people want to do life by their design. God desires that we trust His design and remain in His will. It is far better to trust God and rest in the perfect will of God, rather than to be a part of what God will permit. Just because God permits it, doesn't mean it is perfect. Remember all that God does, it is done well.

Jesus prayed a prayer that I am sure you know of. It is the Our Father Prayer. In this prayer there is a verse that you need to look at very closely. It states:

"Thy kingdom come, thy will be done on earth as it is in heaven."

This verse shows us that there is a heavenly will that God desires to happen on the earth realm. This is also true for our lives. God has a heavenly will for each of us that he wants manifested on the earth realm, however, it will not happen if we do not remain in His will. To remain in the will of God means we have to remain in an intimate relationship with God. We build intimacy with God through avenues of prayer and His Word. This is important to do because we will not know the will of God outside of communicating with Him. How will we know what God wills for us, if we don't seek Him to find out? As mentioned before, we need to live a life of prayer, meditating on the Scriptures, fasting, worship and living a holy life set apart to him. In doing so, God reveals His will to us. Do not expect God to bless "your will" be done. God wants us to come into agreement with His will and therefore we will be blessed beyond measure.

God takes us through processes before He grants extraordinary blessings. He doesn't want us to miss any important sections of the process, because if we do, then we may risk not being prepared enough for the places He will send us. Step by step, God will help us to deal with the process to the destined place of extraordinary blessings. This preparation includes remaining in the will of God. Let today be your day of surrender to the Lord as we determine ourselves to remain in His will and not ours.

Heavenly Father, you are perfect in all your ways. Sometimes I desire to do things my way, rather than to remain in your will. Lord, you know all about my life, purpose and destiny which includes extraordinary blessings. Help me to be obedient to your leadership, to follow your instructions and to remain in your perfect will. You are the Good Shepherd and you know best for me. This I pray in Jesus name Amen.

Winning with **Wisdom**

We have been instructed in the book of Psalms 111 vs. 10a that:

"The fear of the Lord is the beginning of wisdom"

When we learn to reverence and respect the Lord first in all things, we are entering in wisdom. Although the dictionary may define wisdom as ***"good sense"*** or ***"accumulated knowledge"*** wisdom far exceeds these definitions. Wisdom exclusively belongs to God who shares slivers of it to whom He desires. **God is the All Wise One who knows all things.**

Briefly put, wisdom is divine information hidden in the realms of the spirit that we know not of unless it is revealed unto us by the Living God. However, God has a way of revealing this ***"hidden knowledge"*** to whom He pleases. Mankind is always on a discovery to gain more knowledge and at times believes he is the owner of knowledge. This is incorrect. It is God who uncovers hidden information to mankind in the seasons He desires.

Let me give an illustration. If a person has been blindfolded and led in a dark room to sit down that person has no idea of the contents within the room. Now if the blindfolds were still left on when the lights were turned on, the person still doesn't see what or who is in the room because their eyes are still covered. But as soon as the blindfold is taken off and the person can see clearly, the person realizes that they were seated in a decorated room. At the back of the room, there stood a few friends waiting patiently for the unveiling. This is what the wisdom of God does. He is the One who turns on the lights in our Spirits and removes the blindfolds from our spiritual eyes and mind. It is then and only then we gain new information that was originally hidden from us. ***Wisdom is the unveiling of God's divine knowledge.*** When we are empowered with it and use it well, then we will win with it.

Not everyone has the blessing of wisdom. Many people have knowledge, but not everyone is privileged enough to have much wisdom. When God reveals information to us which He can also block from others, we are on the winner's team. God desires for us to be winners and He wants His people to get ahead. He has a way of showing us beforehand what may come and He can direct us on what to do and how to prepare for it. God wants us to ask Him for wisdom for He is the All Wise One. There is none wise like God, neither will there be any wiser than HIM. If you want to win with wisdom, ask God for wisdom. He will grant you a measure of it. Amen.

Heavenly Father, because you are the All Wise Omniscient One, we come to you asking you to grant us wisdom. We need wisdom Lord to win and to move forward to accomplish your will. Lord, we accept by faith, the measure of wisdom that you will allot to us his day and always in Jesus name Amen.

Saying No to an **X-rated** Life

The X-rated life is a life of indecency, perversion, sexual lewdness and derogatory behavior. It is evident now, more than ever and sadly, these behaviors have entered the church.

We witness "x-ration" in movies, hear it in music, men degrade women, women abuse men, and even children are disrespectful and belligerent to parents and authorities. The movement of "x-ration" has become the norm and it is taking over the minds of humankind, but there is hope.

Jesus Christ did warn us that these things would occur before His return. Mankind would be lovers of themselves rather than loving God and others. There would be idolaters, whoremongers, liars, fornicators, adulterers, foolish indecent chatter, drunkards, and murderers etc. In other words, people will have the tendency to lean towards the life that mocks and disregards God, rather than the life that honors God. The bad news is this: A life lived that mocks and disregards God is not a life at all. It's all death and it eventually catches up on the person who chose to live an "X-rated" life.

I have ministered to many women who spoke to me about the indecent things that they have done that clawed endlessly at their inner being. Whether it be involving themselves in orgies, abortions, getting high, prostituting their bodies, bootie calls, stealing etc. the one thing I have noticed is this: ***It hurts their spirit and often times they end up with deep spiritual wounds that only a physician of the Spirit can heal. That physician is Jesus.***

The point is this: The X-rated life is never worth it. Why? When a person gets involved and do things that burden their Spirit man, they end up spiritually sick because they were never designed to carry the weight of sin. The X-rated lifestyle burdens an individual with the weight of sin, but there is hope. Our hope has a name. His name is Jesus Christ, our Savior, Lord and Christ who can move the mountains. He is mighty to save, deliver and heal.

The X-rated life never builds anyone up. Satan uses this type of life to steal, kill and destroy the lives of people who may be unconsciously unaware that it is satan who desires to kill them. This type of life harms a person's spirit first and then attacks their body either slowly or viciously. The x-rayed life can be defined as slow suicide. It is satan who is the craftsman behind the X-rated life and he indulges people to slowly gratify their flesh at the expense of their soul. When a person agrees with satan's contract of death for their life, then he will take it. You have a choice to say no. Don't allow satan to use your weaknesses, seductive snares and appetites of lusts to snatch your life. Remember he is cunning and his ways may seem good and pleasing to the eyes and senses but his ways are never good.

If you realized that you have entered a snare of the x-rated life and you want out and you are ready to say no to satan, this is your time for deliverance. It takes an open heart to receive the promises and deliverances of God. God will not force Himself into a heart that is closed to HIM.

Heavenly Father, I need you. I need the power of your love to extract me out of the deadly snares of satan. I need your power to deliver me from this x-rated life. I need you to root out of my spirit everything that doesn't express your holiness or your Holy Spirit. I need to be made whole. Cleanse me. Mold me. Touch me. Heal me. And make me new again. Come into my heart. I open my heart to you Lord. Do a new work in me and make me whole. This I pray in Jesus name Amen, Amen and Amen.

Young *at Heart*

This topic may be a challenge for many "adults" to absorb because it will test your inner child to come out and play!!! I have always loved observing children. I marvel at their innocence and freedom. If you take the time to observe children, you will find that most of them are certainly not "caught up" with the issues of adults. This is an obvious observation because children don't have the responsibilities of adults, but we can choose to bring out the inner child and simply be *"young at heart."*

We can learn a lot from children. Most of them are playful, energetic, curious, innocent and so much more. We were once children, and I know for sure that I was very energetic and playful! Were you playful, energetic, free, and curious as a child? I have noticed that many adults have lost the connection with their "inner child" and have entered a never ending maze of being serious all the time. This I have learned can be a dangerous detriment to our mind, spirit and soul. When we suffocate the child in us, we get sick quicker and often times commit slow suicide because life consumes us slowly with its cares.

You may want to close this book now because you may think this is not relevant to you. Go right ahead. I can't stop you, but I tell you this: It is well worth it to laugh, smile, love and play again. It is worth it to be young at heart and let go of the burdensome life!

You may ask: With all the responsibilities I have, who has time to play? With all that is on my plate how can I play? You may say: I don't even know how to play anymore. This is where I can help you. You have to relearn how to play. You need to shift some responsibilities to the back of the list, walk away from it for at least three hours and take time to play. You must be determined to create space and time in your life to invite play to come in. Give yourself the blessing of having fun and not feel guilty. It will help you in more ways than you originally thought. If you can't play or find time to play, then you are inviting life to rob you of enjoyment. I like to think of it this way: ***All work and no play is not a balanced life after all!***

Choosing to wake up your inner child to have fun will not be the easiest thing to do, but when you start you will love it and want to do it more. You will also start feeling better in your body and mind.

Playing takes many forms. Take a long nice walk in nature and stop and smell the flowers. Lay down in the grass and enjoy the sun warm up your face. Watch some ants in the garden. Listen to the birds sing. Play with your spouse in bed tickling him or her till they laugh uncontrollably. Play a bible trivia game at church. Play with your children as they jump rope or play cards or a video games with them. Listen to music loud and dance up a sweat. Race or play a game of football with your friends. Play tag or hide and seek with your children or spouse. The opportunities to play are endless and fun! You will have a great time and you will do a great rejuvenation in mind, body and soul! God wants His children to lighten up and live life to the fullest and this includes playing! Let today be the day, you take time to PLAY and be youthful in heart.

Lord, life can get demanding and cluttered, but you desire that we live life abundantly and balanced. Teach us how to reconnect with our inner child and help us to relax and be playful. Rejuvenate our hearts to become youthful as we love you and the life that you have blessed us with. Help us to make the most of this life. This we pray in Jesus name Amen.

Conclusion

Proverbs 14:8 "The wisdom of the prudent is to understand his way.."

It is my prayer that you have gained much hope and wisdom within this book. I have shared with you what the Lord has placed on my heart as it relates to different topics that many people have struggled with, including myself. God wants us to keep our hope in Him for His return is near. We are to reverence Him and to love Him above all else. We will see our lives transform spiritually and other beautiful happenings will manifest thereafter.

I decree and declare that wisdom will reign upon you, in you and through you, as you hold on to hope in our Lord Jesus Christ. Live in His grace and steep yourself continually in prayer and the Word of God as you experience His love and favor daily in Jesus name Amen.

Jesus is Lord!

Loving you.....

Sister Heather Hope

Proverbs 16: 16a
"How much better it is to get wisdom than gold!"